Tunes on a Penny Whistle
A Derbyshire Childhood

Doris E. Coates

ALAN SUTTON PUBLISHING

DERBYSHIRE COUNTY COUNCIL

First published in the United Kingdom in 1993 by
Alan Sutton Publishing Ltd · Phoenix Mill · Far Thrupp
Stroud · Gloucestershire
and Derbyshire County Council · Matlock · Derbyshire

First published in the United States of America in 1993 by
Alan Sutton Publishing Inc · 83 Washington Street · Dover · NH 03820

British Library Cataloguing in Publication Data

A catalogue record for this book is available from the British Library

ISBN 0-7509-0434-8

Library of Congress Cataloging in Publication Data applied for

Cover photograph: *A children's party in Derbyshire, c. 1911.*
(Mr and Mrs F. Winfield)

To my nephew, Michael Dawson,
at Laurel Cottage

Typeset in 11/12 Bembo.
Typesetting and origination by
Alan Sutton Publishing Limited.
Printed in Great Britain by
The Bath Press, Avon.

CONTENTS

INTRODUCTION

This account is based on my memories of rural life during the First World War and its aftermath. Though it is set in a Derbyshire village, it is of more than local significance. The picture portrayed could be equally true of a village in the Welsh valleys, or in the small spinning or weaving communities of Yorkshire or Lancashire.

Here one would find parishes that were not full of pastoral scenes based on farming, under the patronage of the land-owner in the big house. They were outposts of industry, engaged in occupations usually centred on towns. The social structure was different, but they were close-knit communities, sharing the problems and pleasures of their age.

Working people then had few of the rights we have taken for granted today. There was no protection against bad employers, no unemployment pay or sick pay, no right to free medical care or secondary education, a limited electoral franchise and a tiny old-age pension at the age of seventy.

This sounds grim, but it was not a generation of miserable people. There was courage and resourcefulness, and often a great capacity for fun and simple pleasures. Self-help and mutual support was the order of the day and everyone worked together to alleviate hardship through such organizations as Friendly Societies, mechanics institutes, burial societies and nursing associations. The practical benefits of these organizations were usually combined with social pleasures. Then, of course, there were the churches and chapels, and sports and pastimes. Perhaps in most communities there were characters like my father, always ready to take the lead and inspire others to greater effort.

I write this partly in tribute to this remarkable man who was always in the forefront of any activity. He worked long hours in a shoe factory, but lived life to the full, finding equal satisfaction in cycling round the surrounding villages collecting news items for the local press, conducting choirs, public speaking, taking parties of children for picnics, or playing his organ or tin whistle.

These country people hoped to combat social ills by industrial action, or through political movements, but they realized that only education would provide the key to a better future. It fell to their offspring to break down the barriers to this and to pave the way for better chances for others.

CHAPTER ONE

Cottage Memories

Barlow for gentlefolk,
Calver for trenchers,
Middleton for rogues and thieves
and Eyam for pretty wenches.

traditional Derbyshire rhyme

'Horse-manure – 20p ber bag'. The sign was at a field gate in Wiltshire, but my mind was carried back over seventy years to my Derbyshire village of Eyam, when it was a minor triumph to be first on the scene with a shovel and bucket to clean up after the greengrocer's horse and carry off our prize to the vegetable plot.

In those days there were many opportunities to collect such booty. It was not until 1918 that the internal combustion engine had any impact on our lives, so we relied almost entirely on horses. Farm carts were a familiar sight in the village as they carried hay, turnips, potatoes or manure to and from the fields, or pulled up in front of one of the village shops to collect stores. The doctor did his rounds in a pony and trap. A great variety of goods was delivered to our doors. The baker and the butcher would arrive several times a week with their small, high-covered traps; grocers delivered even small orders on their open drays which were similar to those used by the coal man. Then there were the greengrocers. The regular one came twice a week, pulling up at each cluster of houses and announcing his arrival with a shout of 'Apples a pound, pears ninepence', a cryptic remark for all seasons. His fruit and vegetables were piled on his dray, resembling a mobile market stall. We looked out for the first red apples of the autumn, and the appearance of oranges just before Christmas, and tomatoes in high summer. We never had 'out-of-season' produce, and perhaps this heightened our appreciation. Most exciting were the occasions when there was a glut of fruit in Sheffield market. Growers had no freezing or canning firms to take

A view of Town End from the Causeway

their surplus products, so they were bought dirt cheap by traders who would then hawk them round the country villages. They would stop in the lanes, the drays piled high, perhaps with 3 lb baskets of almost over-ripe strawberries, and be surrounded by bargain-hunting housewives. Soon the village would smell of jam-making from end to end. Plums, blackcurrants, or raspberries would all arrive in the same way, with a bonus of cheapness for these thrifty families.

The fishmonger with his cart was a weekly visitor, his wares remarkably fresh after a night journey by express train from Hull to Sheffield, slow train to Grindleford and a leisurely clip-clop of the horse the last 3½ miles in plenty of time for midday meals in Eyam.

More occasional callers were the rag-and-bone men, who usually gave us a donkey stone (for whitening steps) in return for our offerings, and the pot cart, piled high with cups, saucers, plates, brown earthenware stewpots and pudding dishes, chamber-pots and pancheons, usually 'seconds' bought in bulk by the dealer from one of the Staffordshire potteries, and sold very cheaply. So most of the fun of shopping could be enjoyed just a few yards

The road leading to Town End (the village square). The people are standing outside
Furnace's grocers. Furness Wood is in the background

from home, and while the women, shawls round their shoulders, gossiped
and haggled, neither horses nor driver seemed in any hurry.

Public transport depended on the railway, and the nearest station was
Grindleford on the Dore and Chinley line (between Sheffield and
Manchester).

Two families of 'bus' proprietors ran horse-drawn vehicles to meet the
trains. These were of two types, the smaller one-horse 'fly', in which half a
dozen people could sit inside, sitting sideways in two rows, knee to knee,
and the larger 'chara-banc', brought out in the summer for tourists. This
was higher and had an open top with rows of seats facing forward, and
could carry a dozen people on the level. But the steep hill from Grindleford
Village, up past Flora Corner was too much for the two horses with a full
load. It was said that one driver used to charge three different fares, and at
the bottom of the steep hill he would shout, 'First class passengers sit still,
second class passengers get out and walk, third class passengers get out and
shove!'.

My parents and their friends could ill afford bus fares as well as train fares,
so on the rare days out to Sheffield we would spend an hour walking to the

station, get a cheap day return ticket on the train, and only ride on the bus on our return journey if we had a heavy load of shopping.

The first sign of modernization came to the village in 1919. George Marples, one of the bus owners, was a neighbour of ours. He was a dedicated horseman, and when he was called up he joined the cavalry and cared for some of the last horses to be used by the British in battle. He also learned to drive a motor, so when he was demobbed and got his gratuity he decided to buy the first motor vehicle to run the service to the station. We called it a 'bus', but it was very little bigger than the modern estate car. We watched him walk past our window each morning as he set off to get his bus out for the morning journey, with a straw between his teeth and a whip under his arm just as when he had his horses.

Such are my recollections of childhood in Eyam, where I lived with my parents and young brother in a typical picturesque stone cottage, with red rambler roses around the door, a tiny lawn, a cherry tree and a bright cottage garden. It was always called Laurel Cottage, after the large laurel trees in one corner of the garden. It had an earth privy across the lane, no water, gas or electricity and one fire in the living room as the sole source of heat. Like most of our neighbours we were poor, but such were the characters of both of my parents, proud, and courageous, that on the whole we found life good.

I remember my father, Henry Dawson (always known as Harry) as a tallish angular man, with a ginger moustache, his hair already streaked with grey. He worked for a miserable wage in a shoe factory in the village, from 6.00 a.m. to 6.00 p.m. during the week, and 6.00 a.m. to 1.00 p.m. on Saturday. (After 1914 I believe work started at 7.00 a.m.)

This would seem to have left very little time for leisure, but he somehow fitted in a wide range of activities. He was correspondent for the *Derbyshire Courier* for Eyam, and for six other villages. This entailed travelling round to collect news items and a good deal of writing, literally burning the midnight oil. Sometimes articles of topical interest would appear with his initials. He took a leading part in many local organizations. He was chairman of the local Liberals, and an active member of the Eyam Lodge of the Oddfellows Friendly Society, and organized The Eyam Variety Entertainers concert party. Every Sunday he played the organ at chapel in the little hamlet of Froggatt, 4 miles away, and he was always in demand to train and conduct choirs for Sunday school anniversaries and other special occasions throughout the area. As a dedicated temperance worker, he ran the Band of Hope and was held in high regard as a public speaker on the subject. It must have been a busy life, and I now find it amazing that he still devoted so much attention to his family. He worked at anything which would help stretch our meagre income. He gathered wood and sawed it

Laurel Cottage, Eyam. C.1920.

into logs, he rented land a mile away on which to grow vegetables, and did casual farm work to obtain a winter store of potatoes.

He was handicapped by partial deafness caused by a blow on the ear when he was a schoolboy. He had attended the village school till the age of twelve, and for the rest was self-educated. His school exercise books show that his later achievements were built on a sound foundation of geography, arithmetic and English. Reading, writing and spelling were of a high standard, and he was even taught sentence construction and the Latin roots of words. He owed much to Richard Owen, who was still headmaster of the school in my own schooldays.

Harry did not marry until he was thirty-five, but stayed on in the cottage with his parents until their deaths, and then with his unmarried sister, Emma. Though his almost fanatical attachment to his birthplace prevented him from leaving the village in search of better conditions, he was not without a sense of adventure. In the early 1890s he bought the first bicycle to be used in the village, then persuaded several of his friends to do the

George Dawson (1840–98), an amateur music teacher and choirmaster. The author's grandfather

Ann Dawson (1832–98), formerly Ann Bradshaw, descended from the famous Derbyshire family of that name. The author's grandmother

same and form a small cycling club, with their own engraved badge. With such low incomes this must have entailed a great deal of effort and thrift.

The shoe factory always closed for Wakes Week, giving the workers an unpaid holiday. It was a time of extra hardship, and few people thought of going away. In the year of Queen Victoria's Diamond Jubilee Harry determined to visit London. So, August 1897 saw him and 'Little Alan Slater' setting off on their solid-tyred bicycles on the 180 mile journey. They duly arrived there, marvelled at the sights, and cycled back in easy stages. It must have been an unusual project in those days, especially coming from a community of people who rarely travelled even to the next town.

Harry now began to pioneer the idea of saving throughout the year for holidays, and in 1900 he and his friends made the first of several trips by train and boat to the Isle of Man. In more than one way it opened up a new world, for it was on one of these visits that he first met Margaret Corkish, who he was to marry five years later.

At this time Margaret was helping to manage the George Hotel in Castletown, Isle of Man. She had been in domestic service all her working life, first as a nurse-maid, then with varying degrees of responsibility in other households. She apparently never suffered the humiliations and hardships we have come to associate with 'below-stairs' life in Victorian England. This may have been partly due to the lack of class-consciousness in the Manx people, and partly to her own personality. She spoke only of the friendship and appreciation of her employers.

Remembering her love of books and her talents as a letter-writer, it is surprising to realize how little formal education she had received. There was no compulsory education in the Isle of Man in the 1880s, but her mother managed to send her to a Dame School in Douglas, where a little old lady taught a small group of youngsters. One Monday, when she was seven years old, she forgot to take her fee of one penny, and was punished by being caned. She left and refused to attend school for years. Her pleasures then were playing on 'The Strand' and reading, to the delight and surprise of her mother, who had started work at the age of seven and never learned to read. Margaret appears to have gone to another school at the age of twelve, and impressed her teachers with her natural ability. But at thirteen she had to start earning her living.

Margaret was thirty when she came to Eyam as a bride, fair and blue-eyed. Her humour and enthusiasm and continuous ripple of conversation in the lilting Manx brogue were like quicksilver in that Derbyshire setting. But she was soon part of the pattern of village life, sharing work and hardship and pleasures. It was a hard life, but Margaret addressed it with gaiety, and it seemed that her strength increased as difficulties got greater. She performed

Margaret with her mother in the
Isle of Man before her marriage
to Henry Dawson

miracles of housekeeping on our tiny income, and created 'home' in its
truest sense in our ancient cottage.

The cottage had one large living-room, a small stone-floored room used
for storage, and a tiny kitchen and pantry. Upstairs there were two
bedrooms. Normally the door stood open, except in the coldest weather.
There was no entrance hall. The door from the garden led straight into the
living-room, with its oak-beamed ceiling and small windows set into its
yard-thick walls. The room was dominated by a big black-leaded range,
which was the only facility for heating and cooking. It was used for the
kettle, frying-pans, and saucepans and on wash-day a great iron fish-kettle,
in which 'whites' were boiled, balanced there perilously. Accidents were not
infrequent. Then the room would be filled with acrid steam as the fire was
extinguished by the soapy water.

On one side of the fire was the 'boiler', a square container kept full of
water. It never actually boiled, but when the fire was going well a tepid,
rusty brew could be ladled out for personal washing. The lid of this formed
the hob on which the kettle stood when not in use. On the other side was
the oven with three heavy iron shelves. There was usually an appetizing
smell of puddings, stews or bones simmering for broth. On Fridays there

Laurel Cottage cooking range

was much struggling with flues and expert stoking up to get the temperature high enough for the weekly baking of bread and cakes.

On top of the oven, jam jars filled with infusions of medicinal herbs, or mixtures of brimstone and treacle were at hand for anyone with symptoms of illness. The tiny kitchen had a stone sink but no running water. Drinking water was carried daily in buckets from a tap in the village square, a quarter of a mile away, and uphill. It was stored in a red earthenware pancheon (a tall jar), covered with a wooden lid. A rain-water butt, outside near the coal-house, usually provided water for baths, scrubbings, laundry and so on. This would fail in a spell of dry weather. As many as twenty bucketsful had to be fetched on the night before wash-day. This was often my job, sometimes with an old-fashioned wooden yoke across my shoulders with two buckets suspended, and sometimes one bucket at a time, changing every few yards from one aching arm and cramped hand to the other.

Paraffin lamps were our only lights until gas was piped to the village in the 1920s. Candlesticks were carried upstairs to light us to bed. Bedrooms were unheated and bitterly cold in the severe Derbyshire winters. The tiny window-panes would often be opaque with the fernlike etching of frost, and the water in the ewer filmed with ice. But the feather-beds were cosy, and stone hot-water bottles, wrapped in flannel, kept our feet warm, even if they encouraged the chilblains which tortured us.

There was no bathroom, so we each had to wait until members of the opposite sex were out, or in bed. The door was locked and the big galvanized iron bath was installed in front of the living-room fire. Heating the water, and filling and emptying the bath were laborious chores, but there was almost luxurious comfort in washing in that cheerful warmth, and using towels which had been kept warm on the fire-guard.

On one side of the garden was a stile made of horizontal stone slabs. We would climb this and cross the lane to reach a wooden gate leading to the vegetable garden. At the farther end of this was an earth closet and an ash-pit. Having to use this was, perhaps, our greatest hardship. It was unbearably cold in winter, and a treacherous journey in the dark. In summer no amount of disinfectant powder could counteract the smell. At intervals of two or three months council workmen came with a horse and cart and shovels to empty ash-pits and closets. Even inside with all the doors and windows shut the smell was overwhelming.

By modern standards the cottage might be thought to be a poor place but we were all fiercely proud of it, especially my father as his family had lived there for at least four generations. Margaret, my mother, was adept at creating a style and quality of life which overcame the lack of facilities and shortage of money.

Margaret Dawson (née Corkish) as a young woman

The big wooden table in the living-room served for all purposes. In the morning, when the vegetables were prepared on it, or the fire-irons or silver cleaned, it was covered with shiny American oil-cloth. At meal-times a starched white or check table-cloth was laid, with the cutlery and condiments correctly arranged, even while we children were young and clumsy. In the afternoon it might be used for baking, ironing, or preparing fruit for preserves. But when the work was done it would be draped with a thick chenile cloth of red or green trimmed with round bobbles, with a vase of wild or garden flowers or an aspidistra plant in the centre. Such was the fashion of most of our neighbours. It was an assertion of self-respect, like the clean apron or dress and thorough toilet the housewives found time for before tea-time.

I used to think that this was the way ladies lived. I was shocked when one day I called for a school friend and found the family drinking from mugs, with the table covered with newspapers. This was so unusual that I was convinced that they must be very poor indeed, though I later realized that they had much more money than we had. We just refused to behave as if we were poverty-stricken.

CHAPTER TWO

Simple Pleasures

Teach us delight in simple things
and mirth that knows no bitter springs.

Rudyard Kipling, 'The Children's Song'

In recalling times past there is a temptation to paint a rosy picture of happy childhood, with everything cosy and sunny. That would mean ignoring the uglier side of poverty and the continuous struggle to come to terms with it. Of course there was hardship and deprivation. There was the humiliation of wearing clothes fashioned from other people's 'cast-offs', picked up for a few coppers at jumble sales. The subject of footwear caused sore resentment. Thick black stockings we all took for granted, but while some of my friends had laced-up boots of soft leather, mine were heavy and clumsy boy's boots from the local factory which specialized in army boots. To ensure that they lasted as long as possible, steel studs were nailed in the heels and toes. There was much scrimping and saving and a good deal of 'going without'. And yet it is the pleasant memories which I recall with gratitude, when I think of my home.

In the evening the paraffin lamp would be lit and jigsaws, books or simple toys littered the table. On winter evenings my father would try to spend some time with us. He would pile logs on the fire, put scrubbed potatoes in the oven to bake for supper, and teach us tiddlywinks, draughts or simple card-games. He made everything seem tremendous fun. Often neighbours would drop in for a game of whist or a chat, or perhaps to ask for help in filling in an official form or writing a letter. Though we were taught to be mannerly, we were never excluded from the adult circle, so that we learned the pleasures of conversation from an early age.

There was a good deal of story-telling, and since Harry, my father, was an expert in local history, he had a great fund of yarns about the past, about the old lead miners, or ghosts, or the foibles of local characters. It was

Henry Dawson in the year of his marriage, 1905

noticeable that on these occasions he would lapse into a much broader Derbyshire dialect than he used in customary family conversation.

There was enjoyment also in our out-door activities. My father still cycled to neighbouring villages to collect news items for the weekly local paper, but bicycles were not a very common sight on the steep rough roads. From an early age we learned that the logical way to get from one place to another was to walk. Children from Foolow or Bretton thought nothing of the 3 mile walk to Eyam school. People would walk the 7 miles each way to visit Bakewell market, and I remember my mother walking 12 miles to Sheffield when she had missed the train. Walking was a pastime too, and little gaggles of children often set off on this type of activity instead of playing games. We were lucky to have a wide choice of venue: field paths, woods, rocky climbs, lanes, moorlands, hilltops, dales and the banks of streams were all within easy reach, and there were always older girls to help the younger ones if the going got too rough.

We never came back empty-handed. There was always plenty of dead

The Square, Bakewell.
about 1906.

Mam Tor

wood lying under trees. Thin twigs were bundled together for kindling, thicker branches would be dragged, sometimes for miles, to be sawn into logs when we got home. 'Pea-sticks' and 'beansticks' for use in the garden had to be specially selected, and were highly prized. We were experts at finding wild fruit. Hazel-nuts, tiny wild strawberries and occasional raspberries were eaten on the spot, but other country harvests were destined for the family larder. In late summer, groups of mothers and children would spend the whole day on the moors, picking bilberries or cluster-berries. Up there in the boggy patches we gathered great baskets full of sphagnum moss, used by the Red Cross for dressings during the First World War. We were glad that our 2 or 3 mile tramp homeward was all downhill.

Then, of course, there were the wild flowers: primroses, violets, bluebells, marsh marigolds, cowslips, honeysuckle or heather, gathered in their season for the vases at home. Only the may-blossom or hawthorn was forbidden, as it was considered unlucky to take this indoors. Sometimes we were sent to find specific herbs needed for remedies. We knew the habitat of sage, marjoram, eyebright, tansy, camomile, yarrow and comfrey.

The manner of our walk on Sundays was much more restrained. Dressed in our clean Sunday clothes, and usually accompanied by an adult or an older girl, we walked sedately along the road or footpath, and dared not pick up a single twig, for had not the man-in-the-moon been banished there as a punishment for gathering wood on Sunday? On nights of the full moon we had seen him, with his dog at his heel and his bundle of sticks on his back.

Harry loved to walk just for the pleasure of exploring the district and since I was older and stronger than my brother, I was often his companion on these expeditions. By the time I was ten years old I could manage 20 miles in a day, with rests to enjoy our flask of tea and sandwiches. We would climb high to get a panoramic view from Win Hill, Lose Hill or Mam Tor or wander through the villages by the rivers Wye and Derwent. I was infected by his enthusiasm for landscape, for nature study, and above all for history. We walked to the 'Long Barrows' of pre-history, the stone circles of the druids, traces of Roman roads leading to Brough, Norman churches and the ruins of castles, Elizabethan halls and barns where Wesley had preached. We would walk 10 miles to find the only place where lilies of the valley grew wild, in the limestone scree on the steep sides of a dale, or to find secret patches of bee orchids or wild daffodils.

Lack of money or transport were just ignored and we would walk to Castleton to see the Garland Ceremony or to Barlow for a well-dressing. Harry had never seen horse-racing, so one bank holiday he decided to go to Flagg point-to-point races. It was a long journey by road, but he said it was only a dozen miles 'as the crow flies'. We went to Millers Dale and aimed in a straight line from there, up a rocky slope, across rough pastures, over

Children outside Plague Cottage, Church Street. The church tower can be seen in the background

countless dry-stone walls, through thistles and nettles, till we came in sight of the crowds on the course. From our point of vantage on the hillside we saw the whole proceedings at no expenditure whatever.

Life was never monotonous because we set great store on special times and seasons, so that there was always something to look forward to. This was true even of basic things like food. Apples and oranges were enjoyed all the more because we did not see them after Easter until late autumn. Peas were not bought in tins or frozen packets, but appeared in their pods as tokens of high summer. (Dried peas might eke out a winter diet, but they were a poor substitute.) Mince pies were only eaten during the twelve days of Christmas, although a plum pudding might be saved for a birthday or wedding anniversary.

As children, our games, which needed no expensive equipment, followed one another through the year by inscrutable laws of succession. Suddenly on a spring day a boy would whip his top near his back door. Next day whips and tops would be seen in every lane and alley, and in the school playground. The game would have its season, and just as unexpectedly would disappear, and marbles would be all the rage. Boys and girls alike went about all day with calico bags of potties and shooters and blood alleys. The favourite form of this game entailed drawing a circle about a foot in diameter, into which every player put a marble. (Any number could play if the circle was large enough.) Crouching on the ground, the players in turn aimed their glass shooters towards the ring by flicking them along the ground between the thumb nail and the bent index finger. The object was to win your opponent's marbles by knocking them out of the ring. The game ended when the ring was empty, the winner gaining a bulging bag of marbles and everyone getting very grubby knuckles.

After marbles came hoops, big ones, smaller ones, iron ones, wooden ones saved from other years, metal ones from discarded barrels. With sticks of all types and sizes we bowled them the length of the village. It would not be possible today, for neither road nor pavement would provide a safe race-track.

Then the girls would bring out their shuttlecocks and battledores, while the boys impeded the walkers with their improvised trolleys made from pairs of old wheels and a plank. Then it was the skipping season, and even if we could not afford a proper rope with wooden handles we could beg a couple of yards of clothes-line. Communal skipping was best of all. Some adult could usually be persuaded to lend us a long heavy rope, then with a 'turner' at each end, the rest of us would see how many times we could skip in the middle, and we would chant traditional rhymes as we skipped.

Other singing games were popular with the girls in summer. 'Nuts in May', 'Oranges and Lemons', 'Looby Loo', 'Bingo was his Name-O' and 'Mary was a-weeping' are the ones I remember most clearly. The boys

Henry's organ

would be playing cricket, with three chalk marks on a wall for wickets, and a single bat, often home-made. Rounders was played by boys and girls together on cooler days. The server would use a soft ball which the strikers would hit with an open hand, the 'stations' or posts being agreed marks on nearby buildings or garden walls.

Then, of course, there were conkers in autumn, and in winter there was sliding, snowballing and sledging down the steep lanes on various home-made structures. The blacksmith would usually add irons for the runners of the more adventurous who liked speed. There always seemed to be long periods of heavy snow in the Peak District, and I have memories of deep drifts, blocked roads and the village isolated.

The men and boys had their football and cricket teams, and we would go to watch home matches, which were literally uphill and downhill games, as there was not a flat field in the parish. Any cricket ball travelling beyond the actual square careered down a steep slope into a boggy gulley for a certain four. Harry had been a goalkeeper when he was younger, and he used to boast that his football team had defeated Sheffield Wednesday when that team still held amateur status.

We celebrated special seasons and special days. Though today we think little of Sunday observance, there was a good deal to be said for making one day of the week different from all the others. All tools of work were put out of sight; coal, firewood, water and vegetables were brought in on Saturday, and only essential cooking and chores were done. We wore our best clothes and went to chapel, or church and to Sunday school, but most of all it was a family day, enabling fathers particularly to spend time with their children. Sunday lunch was an eagerly anticipated occasion, when we all sat down together and ate the best meal of the week, always including Yorkshire pudding and gravy. At Sunday tea, about five o'clock, we used the best china and a clean damask cloth, and my mother usually produced some delicious surprise of cake or fruit preserve to make it feel like a party. We were not permitted to go out to play, but Harry played the organ or took us for decorous walks. Then we had our books and jigsaw puzzles, and often friends called for a cup of tea and a chat. When our finances were at their lowest we broke the rules a little, and made pots of tea to sell to the ramblers who were then allowed to eat their sandwiches in our garden. Sometimes they would be hungry, and buy a tea of boiled eggs, bread and jam and cake, so there would be a little more profit on the transaction.

The day of the year when we got most customers was the last Sunday in August, known as Wakes (or Plague) Sunday. Every town and village in Derbyshire and Lancashire has its own Wakes Week, often dating back to medieval fairs, and traditionally schools, factories and so on are closed for annual holidays. In the early years of this century work people were not paid for this period so it was a mixed blessing.

Wakes Sunday in Eyam is a day still celebrated today as a commemoration of the heroism of the plague-stricken villagers who isolated themselves to prevent the Great Plague ravaging the surrounding country in 1666. Of a population of 350, 260 died of the plague. We all used to attend the open-air service, held in Cucklet Dell, where the inhabitants went to listen to the Revd Mompesson all those years ago. Thousands of people came from all over the country, as they still do today, to take part in the procession through the streets, led by the vicar and the church choir, and Eyam Brass Band.

But to us children Wakes chiefly meant the fairground, with its roundabouts and swings and hoopla stalls, the smell of naphtha flares, and

The Plague Service, 1913

the rattle of coconuts and the hammer and bell of the strong men's tower. We had little money to spend, but the sound of the organ was a magnet that drew us irresistibly to ride on a horse or a cockerel. We bought bags of brandy-snaps or ginger nuts, and gazed spellbound at the giant steam-engine that powered the machinery, and which would later haul it away to the next stop of its annual circuit.

Many of our customs were connected with the Christian festivals. I need say little about Christmas, as the yule log, carol singers, and stocking-hanging are universally known. At Easter my mother would tint our Easter eggs and inscribe our names on them, before boiling them for breakfast. On Easter Monday we had a 'shake-bottle', a custom I have found nowhere else. It consisted of a medicine bottle in which some hard liquorice, or 'Spanish Juice' was dissolved in hot water. To this we added a variety of boiled sweets, cough-sweets or acid drops, or anything friends liked to donate. We took this out on Easter Monday, and spent hours shaking it to try to dissolve the last of the sweets, pausing to sample the flavour and compare it with the concoctions made by other children. By evening we had drunk the lot. Whitsuntide meant new hats, and the first gooseberry tart, and of course all these festivals meant religious services and special hymns to learn.

More secular festivities included Halloween, when the children frightened one another with turnip lanterns and ghost stories, and the young men took advantage of 'Mischief Night' to play such pranks as moving gates, leading horses into neighbours' fields or rattling door-knockers and running away. It was usually good-natured fun, and I remember little real hooliganism, probably because the village 'bobby' was still apt to dispense summary justice on youths who overstepped the law. November the fifth was celebrated not only with bonfires, catherine wheels and rockets, but with treats of treacle toffee and tharcakes (round Derbyshire gingerbreads).

Once I started school other anniversaries appeared in the calendar. On Ascension Day we filed out of school to form a procession through the street before attending a service in church, with the rest of the day a holiday. On Empire Day (24 May) our mothers could watch us as we marched and counter-marched in the school yard with our Union Jacks, singing songs of the Empire, and dancing national dances. It was essential to get a sprig of oak to pin on our dresses on 29 May (Royal Oak Day) for the big boys would be waiting with bunches of nettles to sting the legs of all who failed to wear this emblem of royalist sympathy.

On Shrove Tuesday the church bell tolled at 11.00 a.m. This was the Pancake Bell to tell the housewives to prepare their batter. In school this was a signal for one of the older pupils to persuade the headmaster to go outside on some pretext. The door was then locked on the inside and through the window the boys shouted that they would not let him in unless he promised them the rest of the day as holiday. After a show of reluctance Mr Owen would at last consent, and would be allowed in to dismiss us. Of course the holiday had been arranged all the time, but we still went through this little ceremony every year.

At that time there was a peal of four church bells and they played a significant part in the life of the village. They pealed for weddings and victories and to bring in the New Year. They were tolled for funerals, marked the time of the church service, and a curfew was rung every night. When someone died the Passing Bell was tolled. Its message told parishioners much about the deceased. To begin there would be one toll for a man, two for a woman and three for a child. Then if one counted the next series of tolls this gave the age. Then the tenor bell would toll for about half an hour to bring the mourning to the whole community.

CHAPTER THREE

Mostly About People

Life's a bumper filled by fate,
Let us guests enjoy the feast.

Words of a nineteenth-century glee

If I give the impression that my father and his contemporaries were somewhat eccentric, it may be because, in the remote, but closely knit community in which we lived, with no radio or television, and few opportunities for travel, there was no pressure to conform to current fashions of thought or behaviour or dress. There was scope for a sturdy individualism, and 'character' commanded greater respect than possessions or position.

Though we had no social status, our family were held in high esteem in the neighbourhood. I suppose, first of all, it stemmed from my father's father, a self-taught peripatetic teacher of music. (Years later as a young adult, I was welcomed by the elderly in the villages of the High Peak and Hope Valley as 'George Dawson's granddaughter'.)

Regrettably, he had died before I was born, but his fame lived on. I think he earned his living as a shoe-maker, but his celebrity rested on his skill as an amateur musician. He would walk miles to surrounding villages, teaching singing and conducting choirs and glee clubs. I still have the bundles of music he used to use. Most of it is religious, anthems and cantatas, and a great deal in his careful manuscript. Often he would compose his own tunes, and a few of these survive. Until comparatively recently the carol singers from Eyam Wesleyan Reform Chapel included in their repertoire 'Hark the Herald Angels Sing' to George Dawson's tune, a mock-Handel contrapuntal arrangement in four parts. In retrospect, my father and his family still seem slightly larger than life.

My father's eldest brother, William, I do not remember at all, and I think he must have died when I was an infant. The family were so reluctant to

William Dawson, the socialist rebel

talk about him that I used to fancy that he had somehow disgraced himself. Actually he was a quiet and honourable man, but, as the eldest son, he had left home to live in Bakewell while his parents were still alive, and shocked them all by becoming a member of the Labour party, who were at that time regarded as anarchists or worse! Harry, good Liberal that he was, thought his brother a dangerous revoluntionary. The only relics I have of this progressive uncle is a pile of monthly magazines for the years 1893 to 1900 with his name pencilled on each. When I saw the title 'The British Workman' I hoped to find political overtones, but instead they were full of propaganda against alcohol and for the Bible. There were articles on travel and emigration, other men's work, like firemen, life-boatmen, shoe-makers, railroad builders, and so on. There were 'do-it-yourself' features, book reviews and art represented by such artists as Holman Hunt. It was all very uplifting, and educational in a cosy way. An interesting fore-runner to modern 'mens magazines'!

Emma, my eldest aunt, was seven years older than my father, and was his favourite sister. In 1876, when she was thirteen years old, she was bound apprentice for five years to a local shoe-manufacturer. Her 'indenture' is an impressive legal document, embellished with red seals and a blue and silver stamp for half-a-crown. Among other conditions, she was forbidden to play cards or dice, or to haunt taverns or playhouses, or to contract matrimony during that term. Her wages were 3s. 6d. a week for the first year, rising to 8s. a week in the fifth year. She became master of her craft, and for many years was a forewoman, earning nearly as much as a man. Emma never married, and continued to keep house at Laurel Cottage after the death of her parents, until 1905, when Harry brought his bride home from the Isle of Man. She then went to live with the younger sister Mary at the other end of the village.

I was half afraid of my third aunt, Annie, whose husband, Jossie, was a quiet gentle man, devoted to horses and all other animals. I chiefly recollect

Annie and Jossie in unusually formal pose. Jossie was typically seen with his horse

his strong arms, lifting me on to Blossom's back, or putting me in the loose-box with the calves, much to my mother's alarm. They lived at High Cliff Farm, a mile from the village high up on the Edge. There was a cool dim dairy with stone benches and a fountain, where Annie churned the butter and shaped it into half-pound pats with a swan moulded on the top of each. She was a kindly soul, but had a sharp tongue. Her voice was known to the whole neighbourhood. If the wind was from the west people in the village heard a wail of 'Co up' 'Co up' and knew that Annie was calling in the cattle for milking up on the high slopes.

My three aunts, who had hardly ever been out of the village till they were middle-aged, all ended their days overseas. In 1912 Mary and Emma went to Detroit, USA, with Mary's husband, Uncle Billy Gowland, who had already established himself with a job at Henry Ford's motor factory. Twelve years later, Annie and Jossie, then in their sixties, went to join Jossie's son and his family in Winnipeg, Canada. I was sixteen years of age. They would dearly have loved to take me with them, but I would not desert my parents. A friend took me to Liverpool to see them off. It was like attending a funeral, with the mourned ones being carried to Eternity on a liner, never likely to be seen again.

'Aunt' and 'Uncle' were courtesy titles we children gave to any close friends of my parents who came to see us. The childless ones were glad to adopt us as relatives, and gave us little gifts and sweets, and much encouragement.

There was Little Alan Slater, my father's companion since schooldays, who would sit for hours chatting in the broadest of Derbyshire dialects. Less than 5 ft tall, he would loll in the rocking-chair with his tiny feet barely touching the floor. The waistcoat buttons of his navy suit strained across his chest, on which was displayed a heavy silver chain securing his large pocket watch. The chain jangled with coins and medals, including the silver badge of Eyam Cycling Club. Alan seems to have followed everywhere Harry led and had been his partner in such sidelines as shoe mending, cycle repair and accessories, as well as participating in such enterprises as pioneer cycling and trips to the Isle of Man.

He was a shrewd, humorous man who hated pretension. On their famous cycle ride to London in 1897 they had called at a café and Harry had tried to impress a pretty waitress with charm and fine talk. He loved to tell how Alan had deflated him. 'Dunna thee tek any notice of 'im, lass. He's nowt but a common cobbler like messen.'

Then there was 'Uncle' Farewell Barnes. He was the youngest of a family of fourteen. His mother gave all the twelve girls names beginning with 'F'. At last she had a boy called Frederick, and when another son was born she called him 'Farewell', hoping he would be the final.

The Eyam Cycling Club – 'Little' Alan Slater and Charlie Maddock at an early meeting with Margaret in the Isle of Man

A slight slim figure, with a reedy treble voice and a droopy ginger moustache, Farewell was the village joker. He was able to move with almost feline speed and silence, and he delighted in appearing with disconcerting suddenness to upset the gravity of any serious gathering. He was a near neighbour of ours, and he would often arrive with a great air of urgency and sit on a hard wooden chair just inside the door, and with deadly seriousness would tell the most outrageous tale or make some wildly improbable request. He would invent the most ridiculous errands for us children: 'Go to Ellis's shop and tell them to send Mrs Barnes a new colander as hers leaks', or 'Ask the butcher to send us a sheep's head and tell him to leave the eyes in then it will see us through the week'.

Not all his humour was as 'corny' as that. One escapade fooled the whole neighbourhood for weeks. He was a brilliant mimic, and late one May evening he climbed the Lover's Leap rocks in Middleton Dale and for almost an hour imitated the nightingale, a bird never known to visit that district. He was heard by courting couples, and the next day the phenomenon was mentioned at the shoe factory where he worked. Pleased by his success, he repeated the performance almost every night for a fortnight. News spread and crowds from surrounding villages were gathering in the Dale to hear the unusual visitor. Newspaper reporters and ornithologists arrived, and there were letters in the local press and in more learned journals. Then the singing stopped, and the listeners kept their vigil in vain; it was only when the song was heard actually on the factory premises one dull afternoon that anyone realized that they had all been hoaxed!

Of all my relatives, Uncle Billy Gowland was the most flamboyant. He was the husband of my father's youngest sister, Mary, and though he emigrated to the United States when I was still a small child, I remember him vividly and enjoyed hearing stories of his escapades from my father. He was a burly Irishman with bright red hair and a great ginger moustache. He was full of fine boastful stories, walked with a swagger and laughed and talked so loudly that he was always sure of being the centre of attention. At the local pubs he was immensely popular, unless he ran out of companions willing to treat him, or got fighting drunk. He was a bit of a scamp and avoided the humdrum business of a regular job if he could see a chance of adventure. Naturally he enlisted in the army to go to South Africa to fight the Boers. Billy's return from the war coincided with an event still recounted in family circles many years later, although it happened before I was born.

The coronation of King Edward VII had been arranged for 26 June 1901. In every town and village throughout the country (and no doubt throughout the Empire) plans had been made for celebrations. In Eyam they

Uncle Billy Gowland in Detroit in later life with his wife Mary, in the 1920s

were organizing a splendid parade, to be led by Eyam Brass Band. There was to be dancing in the street, an ox roast in the Town End (the village square) and a bonfire at the top of Sir William Hill, up above the woods at the edge of the moors.

The wood had been gathered and sawn. The ox had been slaughtered and the spit on which it was to roast had been erected by the men of the Coronation Committee. In countless homes the women were cooking batches of Derbyshire oatcakes on their griddles. The dust had been shaken from miles of bunting and flags, last used for the Diamond Jubilee of the 'Old Queen'. The bandsmen had polished their instruments, their wives had brushed and pressed their uniforms. Innkeepers had doubled their stocks of beer, and everywhere activities were at fever pitch.

Then came rumours of disaster. King Edward was seriously ill, and the coronation would have to be postponed. No doubt there was disappointment and confusion, not only in London, where arrangements for this glittering regal occasion had to be halted, but throughout the Empire, where thousands of lesser festivities were cancelled. But in Eyam they were not dismayed. They intended to carry on with their celebrations, coronation or no coronation. Of course it would not do to cheer for a gravely ill king, so an alternative had to be found. Someone mentioned Billy Gowland, and everyone accepted the suggestion with enthusiasm.

The Boer War still dragged on, but some soldiers were on the way home. The news that Billy was due on 26 June was a tremendous piece of luck. Now their celebrations could go ahead as a fitting welcome for the 'hero' coming back from the war. So the fire was lit under the spit, festoons of bunting were hung in every available space, and banners in praise of 'Good Old Billy' hastily replaced the more patriotic 'God Save the King'.

By the morning of the great day the local horse-drawn 'chara-banc' and every other suitable conveyance had been commandeered. Horses and men were fortified for their journey, then the noisy cavalcade set off on the drive to Grindleford railway station. There was the parish council and Eyam Brass Band, in their white uniforms and straw boaters, with new red ties and hat-bands for the occasion. Officers of the Oddfellows Club, wearing their sashes and regalia, and members of the Coronation Committee were all there, with many other men who could cling to the precariously-loaded vehicles. In the leading wagonette were Billy's wife and sister-in-law, Mary and Emma, in flounces and frills and big feathered hats, escorted by their brother Harry. Somewhere room had been found for a barrel of beer and a crate of tankards as emergency supplies for the expedition. Fortunately they reached the station safely, and crowded onto the platform only minutes before the train emerged from the tunnel. A carriage door opened and Billy came out to meet his unexpected reception. There was much cheering and backslapping and jostling to shake the hero's hand. The shouting of the crowd and Billy's uproarious laughter drowned the sound of the departing steam engine. The band played 'See the Conquering Hero Comes' as they made their way to the waiting transport.

The barrel was broached, healths were drunk, then Billy was hoisted onto the leading wagonette next to Mary. So they brought the prodigal home. It was downhill first to Grindleford Village, where everyone came out into the street to cheer them as they went by. Then they started up the long hill to Eyam New Road, raising clouds of dust from the limestone cobbles. At Flora Corner most of the men got down, partly to push the vehicles to help the horses over the steepest part of the journey, and partly to quench their thirsts once more. But Billy sat in state on his high perch, jollying the men and urging on the horses, and revelling in his role of 'king for the day!'

At Jacob's Ladder they all remounted, to travel the last mile with unabated noise and hilarity. Long before they reached Riley Gate they could be heard by those who had been left behind, and a great crowd surged to meet them. The ragged procession came at last to the Town End where Billy was carried shoulder high to an improvised dais and enthroned there, surrounded by the village dignitaries.

After the speeches and cheers there was community singing as the band played 'He's a Jolly Good Fellow', 'Soldier of the Queen' and 'See the

Victory Celebrations included an ox roast, 1919

Conquering Hero Comes', again and again. Neither the singers nor the players seemed quite sure which item they were playing, but the confusion only added to the hilarity. The church bells pealed and the sun shone and the celebrations lasted all day. There was beer in abundance, and everyone ate great helpings of roast ox and Derbyshire oatcakes. The children plaited the ribbons of the maypole and old men clog-danced. Spontaneously a procession formed, and they were led up and down the mile-long village street, led by morris dancers and the band played 'Pudden in a lantern'. Then came Billy, sitting high in his wagonette, acknowledging the cheers and ribald remarks with a somewhat inebriated impersonation of royalty. At night there were torch-lights, and the long climb up Sir William Hill, and fireworks, and the biggest bonfire in living memory. In fact I am told that no festivity in Eyam has ever surpassed Billy Gowland's Coronation.

31

The men of my father's generation were certainly unconventional, so it is not surprising that they took pride in the more eccentric of their ancestors. My father may have derived his love of music from his father, an itinerant singing-master, but he was apt to boast more proudly of his kinship with a much more illustrious musician, Samuel Slack of Tideswell (a village 5 miles from Eyam). Samuel, who was born in 1757, was a celebrated bass singer of some national fame. He was frequently heard in London and was summoned to sing for royalty on several occasions.

When he retired into private life Samuel returned to his native village of Tideswell. He trained and conducted several village choirs in the Peak District, and became the leading spirit in the local 'Catch and Glee Club', which met monthly at the George Inn at Tideswell. One of these meetings is depicted in a picture which always hung next to the organ in Laurel Cottage. It is a lithography by Thomas, from a painting by Potts, entitled 'Life's a Bumper'. In the group with Sammy are the landlord of the George and his wife, the notorious drunken parson of Tideswell and Chadwick of Mottram, a schoolmaster. They are sharing music books, seated at a table with jugs, glasses and long clay pipes, their mouths wide and their faces grimacing as they lustily sing the partsong 'Life's a bumper filled by fate'.

Sammy Slack must have been a great character, for his fame still persists in Derbyshire. Legendary tales of his escapades show him as dissolute and unconventional. His favourite haunt was the beer-house, and it was said that his voice was so powerful that the vibrations shattered the glasses on the shelves. When he went to London in answer to a command to sing before King George his visit culminated in several convivial evenings, and while in a tipsy state he insulted a Guards Officer who then challenged him to a duel. He was too drunk to appreciate the significance of this, and returned to his lodgings to sleep it off. Early next morning he was surprised to be wakened by two red-coated visitors who said their friend had sent them to 'demand satisfaction'. Slack sat up in bed, and with the full power of his voice, sang a verse of his favourite song 'Black-eyed Susan'. 'There' he said, 'that's given satisfaction to thousands, including the king, and its all th' satisfaction tha'll get'. Presumably they were highly satisfied as nothing more was heard of the duel.

Back in Derbyshire Sammy would walk miles to make music and to drink. He trained an amateur group at Barlow about 20 miles from Tideswell. Once he was walking back from there to Tideswell, very late, and again rather drunk. He got safely to Stoney Middleton, but the long haul up the stiff path to Eyam, known as the 'cliff', was too much for him, and he found a hollow and went to sleep. At dawn a deafening bellow wakened him, and a huge bull stood menacing over him. He rubbed his eyes and stared back as it repeated the threatening bellow. 'He mon, that's

'Life's a Bumper' always hung on the wall of Laurel Cottage. It depicts Sammy Slack, the legendary Tideswell singer, with drinking companions. (On the organ, to the left, is the silver cup Harry won for bowls)

nowt! I can go an octave lower than thee!' and he proceeded to do just that. The sound so terrified the bull that it took to its heels and blundered away down the slope towards Stoney Middleton. Samuel Slack died in 1822 at the age of sixty-five, and was buried in Tideswell churchyard. No stone was raised over his grave until 1831 when a memorial was put up at the expense of the amateur members of Barlow choir, assisted by some outside contributions.

Perhaps the most famous reputed ancestor could be traced back through my father's mother, who died in the 1890s. She was a Bradshaw, a poor relation of a family which once held large estates in Derbyshire. She claimed to be descended from John Bradshaw, who was born in 1602 and who lived as a boy in Bradshaw Hall, in Eyam. By the beginning of the twentieth century this was in use only as a barn, but stories persisted of its historic connection with John Bradshaw. It was said that this verse had been found scratched in the glass of one of the windows:

Some Bradshaw cousins

My Brother Harry shall till the land,
My Brother Frank shall be at his command,
But I, poor Jack, shall do that
Which all the world shall wonder at!

'Poor Jack' studied law and eventually became a judge in Wales, and in Cheshire. During the Civil War he supported Cromwell. When Charles I was captured in 1648 the remnants of the House of Commons determined to bring him to trial, though this was constitutionally illegal. This rather obscure Judge Bradshaw was selected to preside. The king refused to plead before the tribunal as he claimed it had no jurisdiction over him, but Bradshaw silenced every legal argument and denied Charles an opportunity to speak in his own defence.

Lord Macauley, the eminent Victorian historian, writes:

That revolutionary tribunal pronounced Charles a traitor, a tyrant, a murderer and a public enemy, and his head was severed from his shoulders before thousands of spectators, in front of the banqueting hall of his own palace! (*History of England*, Macauley, 1873).

Judge Bradshaw

Bradshaw was suitably rewarded for his part in this terrible act of revenge. He was made Chancellor of the Duchy of Lancaster, and became President of the Council, and when he died, in October 1659, he was buried in Westminster Abbey. After the restoration of Charles II in 1660, however, his body was disinterred, together with those of Cromwell and Ireton. The corpses were exposed all day on the gallows at Tyburn, and then re-buried in a common pit near the gallows. So his prophetic verse was true: he had 'done that which all the world had wondered at!'.

CHAPTER FOUR

Making Ends Meet

*Poverty is no disgrace to a man, but it is
confoundedly inconvenient.*

Revd Sydney Smith. 1771–1845

Though there was a light-hearted side to the people of Eyam and their
activities, this was against a background of hardship. It was a poor village. A
few men worked in quarries, and a few farmers scratched a living from the
thin soil in the bleak climate. The same family would run a farm through
several generations. Often it would be a holding of a mere 50 acres of hilly
land, divided into small irregular fields by dry stone walls. One important
farmer had 100 acres, but since one-third of that was moorland, bracken,
outcrops of rock and woodlands, his was still a small-scale activity.

Most of the land was used as pasture for a handful of sheep, a few dairy
cows and beef cattle. There was nothing like the flocks of up to a
thousand sheep which could be seen on the slopes above Hope and
Edale, only 20 miles away. There was no spare money for capital
investment to improve conditions or equipment. There would be a few
poultry and a few pigs, and calves would be reared to be sold as stirks
(yearlings) in Bakewell market. Milk was delivered locally, warm from the
cow, in pint or quart metal cans with lids, from which it was poured into
jugs. If you asked for a 'gill' you would get half a pint. Surplus milk was
put in churns loaded onto a cart and taken to Grindleford station to
catch the train to Sheffield. Most farmers wives churned enough butter
for their own family and perhaps a bit extra to sell locally or take to
market with any surplus eggs.

Some hay was cut for winter feeding, and there were a few arable fields
growing potatoes, oats or mangolds. It was hard work, and the whole
farming family had to work long hours to survive. Few could afford extra
labourers; casual labour would be recruited for haytime, harvest and for

A typical farm scene in the early part of the century

planting and picking potatoes, but this was rarely paid for in cash. A sack or two of potatoes at the end of the season was a customary reward.

Thus there was not sufficient traditional rural work to support the population, and the majority of families were dependent on work in shoe manufacture. During Victorian times great changes had taken place in the pattern of rural life throughout England. Between 1871 and 1890 there was a disastrous slump in agriculture, causing thousands to leave villages either to emigrate, or to find work in industrial towns as labourers, often having to live in slums.

In some areas there was a converse movement and the factories were sited in the villages, creating urban pressures in isolated communities where they were powerless to fight for better conditions. Alien industries like cotton mills were attracted by the availability of water power from the mountain streams in Derbyshire and Lancashire. Tiny villages like Litton and Millers Dale had mills which employed some local labour, but in their early days they relied largely on the iniquitous child 'apprenticeship' system, importing children from distant workhouses. Some mill-owners were good employers by their own rights, but others allowed living and working conditions of gross inhumanity.

Other enterprises, like the boot and shoe factories of Eyam and Stoney Middleton, developed from cottage industries. Individual craftsmen producing hand-made shoes progressed to the use of simple machines, and so were able to employ neighbours and members of their families. Their need of larger premises led to the building of small factories or the adaptation of existing buildings, as is the case of the old school which became West's factory. The factory system was incongruous in these remote rural communities, but it was welcomed at first because it found employment for many who would have had to leave the village after the decline of lead-mining and the closure of the small silk-weaving firms which had flourished for a short period in the later nineteenth century.

In 1895 there were six wholesale boot shoe and slipper manufacturers in Eyam, and a further five in Stoney Middleton. (The development of the industry in Northampton, Leicester and Norwich forced several of these out of business.') By 1910 there were only three 'shoe shops' in Eyam, all making women's and children's shoes and slippers, and the same number in Stoney Middleton making men's heavy boots. They employed most of the female labour of the district, and a smaller number of men. Workmen found it difficult to keep their jobs unless they brought their daughters to work in the factory when they were old enough to leave school.

Since there was no alternative employment, and only destitution for the unemployed, the work people had to endure appalling conditions and starvation wages. (Sixty-three hours work for £1 in 1913, and fifty-nine hours work for 29s. in 1917, when the national average for the job was at least double that amount.) But the employers had a captive workforce, and knew that they could only continue to exist in a competitive market by keeping their costs low.

I can best describe conditions in the shoe factories by quoting from notes written by my father, probably in 1916/17. I do not know why he wrote this, but it may be a draft of a speech. He worked in Ridgeways shoe factory from about 1885 to 1917. During the latter years he was a 'clicker', a job which was considered superior in Norwich or Northampton, but which only carried the minimum wage in Eyam. This account expresses his amazement at early mechanization, and his anger at working conditions:

When the leather is produced, men will cut out from the skins the various parts which comprise the uppers. [Until recent years] this was done by hand with a cardboard pattern and a sharp knife. That is how these men came to be called 'clickers', by continually running the knife along the edge of the table to sharpen it, and the rapidity with which the knife was drawn caused it to make a clicking sound.

Today, ponderous machinery is used for this process. The skin of leather is placed on a large block of wood, and large knives the shape

A cobbler, at the turn of the century

of the uppers are placed upon it, and by touching a lever, part of the machine drops on it and chops the leather out. This process is quick and dangerous. A dozen pieces of leather can be cut out in a minute.

After we have got all the pieces of leather which comprise the uppers (probably 5 or 6 persons have cut the various pieces) we take them on to the Bending room. Here a girl or young woman, who is called a 'Bender' will trim the edges of the various pieces and stitch them together, making the uppers complete. Much of this is done by ordinary sewing machines and two or three girls will have assisted in stitching the uppers together.

We next take the uppers to the 'Rough-cutting room' where the pieces of leather which comprise the soles, insoles and heel pieces are cut out. Heavy machinery is required for this work. Large pieces of leather are placed on a block of wood and knives of the shape of soles and heels put upon them and by the pressure of the machine they are chopped out of the bends of leather. This work is dangerous as persons working these machines are liable to have fingers or thumbs taken off by the machine.

Having got our uppers and all the various pieces of leather necessary we go to the 'Riveting room', where the sole and heel-pieces are rivetted together. Here we see some wonderful machinery. Iron blocks the shape of a foot are used. The insole is tacked on, then the upper fastened to the toe and heel. Then it is taken to a machine called a 'Lasting machine' which in a human fashion pulls the uppers over the insole and at the same time drives a tack to hold it in its place. So wonderfully accurate and quick is this machine that it can drive tacks in as quick as you can count.

Having got our uppers fastened on, the sole is next tacked. Then it is taken to a riveting machine which drives rivets in round the edge of the sole as quick as a sewing machine makes stitches.

All the various pieces which comprise the heel are placed in a groove of the size of the heel. The boot is placed sole down upon the heel pieces, a moveable arm is placed in the boot and a lever pressed by the foot. Rivets are forced upwards through the heel pieces and through the boot, making it secure to the boot.

Our boots are now made, but the edges and soles are rough and unpolished, so we take them to the finishing room. A machine with a circular knife making 1,400 revolutions to the minute soon smooths the edges and heels. After the edges and heels have been inked or coloured they are polished by circular irons revolving at a great speed, the friction of which polishes the fore-part of the boot and the heel.

After describing the finishing processes, Harry then discusses the hours of work. By 1917 these had been reduced to sixty-one-and-a-half hours per week: Monday to Friday – 6 a.m. to 6 p.m. with two half-hour breaks for breakfast and dinner; Saturday – 6 a.m. to 1 p.m. with half-hour for breakfast. There was, of course, no facility for eating in the factory and the operatives literally ran home and had only fifteen minutes to bolt their food, which had to be waiting on the table for them.

The shoe operatives find it difficult to take an intelligent interest in his or her work, and the body, as a consequence of using the same set of muscles every day and others not being called into action, is apt to deteriorate. Girls who sit over a sewing machine become round-shouldered and lose their eyesight by continual straining to look at the fine work before them. Many a time when the light is bad, one of the contemptible actions of our firm is refusing to light up the gas. At early morning or at dusk and during dull days the girls are compelled to burn candles, and purchase the same out of their small wages. These girls are on 'piecework' – that is paid for the amount of work done, and the price paid for the work is most inadequate. Take the case of P.A. ankle straps [a style of shoe made for women and children with a buttoned strap round the ankle}. The girls formerly sewed the upper together and ran the binding leather round once, by machine. They were afterwards sewn over by hand. Handworkers were paid ninepence a dozen pairs, and machinists 1s 1d. Now the girls have to machine them throughout for ninepence a dozen pairs. When the girls require them they bring with them their candles, purchased out of their hard earned wages, and on a dull day the spectacle may be seen of girls working to the flickering light of a candle. Picture to yourself forty machines, each lit by candle power, and reflect that these girls are having to work almost double to earn a bare wage. And the bosses are growing richer day by day, 'pulling down barns to build bigger'. To me the term 'contemptible' is mild to express my sentiments.

The position of the men and boys is not much better. The standard wage is 22 shillings a week [it continued at this sum throughout the 1914–18 war, in spite of the doubling of the cost of living, and much higher wages elsewhere].

This works out at $4\frac{1}{2}d$ an hour, less than an ordinary labourers wage. We now have what is known as a 'checker'. When we come to work at 6 a.m., 9 a.m. or 2 p.m. we check our time on a card, and all the odd minutes are totalled up at the end of the fortnight, and knocked off our wage. When you consider that if you only lost 5 minutes per day, that is an hour a fortnight. Five minutes is a small margin when we are apt to over-lie at 6 a.m., and a bare half hour at breakfast pinches one for time.

Some work is very injurious to the health, especially the buffing and scouring machines. You can understand how the band of sand-paper buffing the bottom or scouring the heels causes particles of leather, sand-paper and fine brass [from the rivets] to get on the lungs of the operative, and very few are able to follow it for long together.

Other machines are dangerous to work. There is hardly a clicker or a rough-cutter who works with a revolution press, but what has lost a finger or thumb, or had them crushed at some time or another.

The monotony of the work too, tells on the operatives and makes them listless. Here is a lad who is inking the edges of boots all day, another is colouring the bottoms, and probably does from 800 to 1000 pairs a day. Does it get monotonous? [These lads might be as young as thirteen years. They were paid about 4s. a week.]

It is this monotony which has taken the life out of the operatives and made them the tools of the manufacturers. If the operatives would combine they could insist on radical reforms and increased wages, but the nature of the work has made many of them inert, so that they do not seem to realize their power, or to have the energy to fight for their rights.

These were brave words, and in course of time Harry was to suffer grievously for his opinions. But in the early years of this century bad working conditions were not the only source of hardship. There were none of the safeguards we take for granted in these days of the Welfare State. There was no National Health Service, so doctor's bills had to be paid, but workers too ill or infirm to work received no income at all.

There was no unemployment pay, and even the annual holiday week, when the factory closed down, meant a week without wages. Any misfortune could bring stark destitution. Often the iniquitous Poor Law and the degrading workhouse were the only alternatives to starvation.

People like my father knew that they had no power to change the system, but they tried to alleviate it through self-help organizations, like Friendly

Church Street with Joe Harrison's newsagent's shop, the Mechanics Institute and the Bull's Head Inn

Societies. My father was a leading member of the local 'Club', 'The Loyal Peak Miner's Lodge of the Manchester Unity of Oddfellows', to give it its full name. When I was a child I was only aware of the outward show, like seeing my father resplendent with the ornate chains of office as Grand Master, or watching the members on parade.

One of the most colourful events in the year was the 'Club Feast', a festival to celebrate the anniversary of the local lodge of the Friendly Society. The procession assembled by the Bull's Head Inn, where the Loyal Peak Miners had their headquarters. It was a strictly masculine occasion, and every able bodied man in the village seemed to be there. Led by a brass band the parade set off for its march up and down the village street.

First came the banner, huge and intricately worked, all silken blue, gold and red, with fringes and tassels. This depicted the symbols of the order: there was Britannia surrounded by the continents, the Royal arms, the arms of the City of Manchester, and above the figures of Faith, Hope and Charity. At the top was a great eye (the all-seeing eye of God) and many other symbols such as crossed keys, an hour-glass, a beehive and a globe. This rich and splendid standard was carried by three men, the centre one with a leather belt with a socket to hold the flagpole, and the others holding the tassels. If there were visiting delegations, other banners would follow, each rivalling the next in the splendour of the design and the beauty of colour.

Then came the men in their Sunday suits and stiff white collars, transformed to figures of pageantry by their regalia. All wore rosettes, and vivid sashes, worn diagonally over one shoulder, varying in colour and design according to their past or present rank in the branch, and aprons edged with coloured braid. In the front rank the Noble Grand Master (the elected chairman for the year) wore his chain of office, a massive arrangement of gilt and jewelled medallions on a stole of blue velvet fringed with gold. The past Grand and the Vice Grand Masters had chains befitting their rank. They made a brave display as they followed the band 'down-town' to the little chapel, then 'up-town' to Town Head, and finally back to the church, to disperse at exactly one o'clock for the feast at the Bull's Head, with a menu of roast beef, Yorkshire pudding, apple pie or Bakewell pudding, and plenty of ale. From their inception friendly societies encouraged brotherhood and colour and conviviality in a drab world, and the annual 'feast' was kept by branches everywhere, usually at Wakes or some other local holiday.

Oddfellows were seen in more solemn procession at funerals of members or their kin. When I was a child, hearses and carriages were used only by the rich, or by families bringing the coffin home from some distant place, so if there was a death in a cottage it was usual for the coffin to be borne on

Harry in later years in the regalia
of the local lodge of the
Manchester Unity Order of
Oddfellows

the shoulders of half a dozen young men who were friends of the family,
from the home of the deceased to the church. Behind would walk the
family mourners, and after them the club members. Two by two, wearing
black sashes, armbands and ties. Often it would have been the club secretary
who had bidden the mourners, arranged the bearers and generally given
comfort to the bereaved family. At the graveside a special service would be
read after the minister had finished the Church of England service.

The sense of brotherhood was fostered by the monthly lodge meetings
which were essential features of all Friendly Society branches throughout
the country. Quite simply the object of the Friendly Societies was mutual
insurance. I quote from the Rule Book of the Stoney Middleton Lodge for
1882:

The business shall be carried on at the 'Lover's Leap Inn', and that it shall have for its object the raising of funds by entrance fees, contributions, fines, donations etc., for the following purposes, – viz:- Rendering assistance when sick and unable to follow their employment, to defray the funeral expenses of deceased members, and of deceased members wives, and affording assistance to members seeking employment.

(See appendix one for further notes on Friendly Societies.)

During the period 1905 to 1912 I have records of the monthly contribution at Eyam of 3s. 4d. a month, and the weekly benefit for a sick member of 8s. a week (4s. for those over seventy or chronically ill). This seems little enough to provide for a family, but it was better than the abject despair of no income at all.

Alongside these sick and funeral benefits many lodges provided 'Medical Attendance'. This enabled members 'on the club' to go to the doctor for free treatment and medicine. Local doctors usually co-operated in the system in exchange for a payment of about 3s. a year per member. In the years before the first National Health Bill this was a revolutionary concept, and it must have saved lives as it enabled men to have medical treatment when they would have been prevented from doing so by poverty.

Of course, when I was a child I did not understand all this. I was familiar with the 'Sick Visitor' who called when my father was ill to give him his meagre 'Club Money'. At those times he didn't dare to chop sticks, or bring in the coal as it would then be thought that he was fit to work, and his money would be stopped. My mother would struggle with all the chores though often in poor health herself. She rarely dared to go to the doctor herself, as women and children were not provided for by the friendly society, and doctor's bills could be crippling. Mothers often delayed seeing a doctor until it was too late, or suffered years of pain and discomfort which could have been relieved if they had had access to early treatment.

It was when I was in my teens, and my father asked me to accompany him when he was a delegate to a conference in London that I really understood what a remarkable scheme of self-help these barely-educated working people had devised. In the 1880s there was a spontaneous grass roots movement in many parts of the country, when angry men, finding that no one cared for their plight, formed little groups to help one another. They met at local inns, often at great risk, as such meetings could be raided on suspicion of treason being plotted. So they had to be secret societies, with secret signs and hand shakes and symbolic knocks. Each 'lodge' devised its own rules, and organized its own finances. Members had to educate

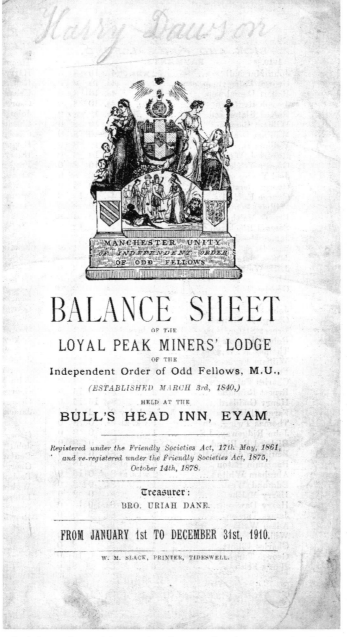

BALANCE SHEET

OF THE

LOYAL PEAK MINERS' LODGE

OF THE

Independent Order of Odd Fellows, M.U.,

(ESTABLISHED MARCH 3rd, 1840,)

HELD AT THE

BULL'S HEAD INN, EYAM.

Registered under the Friendly Societies Act, 17th May, 1861, and re-registered under the Friendly Societies Act, 1875, October 14th, 1878.

Treasurer:

BRO. URIAH DANE.

FROM JANUARY 1st TO DECEMBER 31st, 1910.

W. M. SLACK, PRINTER, TIDESWELL.

The balance sheet of the Loyal Peak Miners' Lodge, giving details of their accounts in 1910

themselves to take an active role, so all had a chance of running for office, presiding at meetings, book-keeping and secretarial skills, managing and investing money.

It is remarkable that without professional help, and with only voluntary subscriptions, the Friendly Societies not only survived, but flourished. It was necessary that men should continue paying their subscriptions throughout their lives, but they would soon have tired of dull meetings just to collect dues and fines. The founding fathers, who incorporated business with social evenings in the upper rooms in the pub, with the play-acting of secret signs and oaths, and the glamour of regalia and ritual, provided a perfect way to ensure the members' loyalty. The formula still works even in these more sophisticated days.

CHAPTER FIVE

Influences

Sabbath Schools are England's glory
Let them spread on every hand.
They send forth the Saviour's story
To the thousands of our land.

Wesleyan hymn, popular about 1910

Looking back, I wonder why most families of my generation managed to live with so much courage and cheerfulness. We certainly suffered greater deprivation than is conceivable today, yet I remember very little crime, hooliganism or vandalism, or any of the ills we now blame on poverty. Homelessness only occurred when ruthless landlords evicted their tenants. Then neighbours and friends were quick to give a helping hand.

But though most cottages were over-crowded and insanitary, it was rare for a youth or unmarried daughter to be turned out of the house, though it was not wise to enquire how many people slept in a room in some large families. It was some relief if children of thirteen or fourteen years left school to go to 'living in' jobs, boys to distant farms as labourers, girls to middle-class homes as domestic servants.

In both cases they would be expected to work very long hours for very little pay, but they were fed and clothed and given a decent bed. However we criticize the way they were exploited according to modern ideas, it must be admitted that in many cases they were better off than if they had stayed at home and found local work. I remember being envious of friends who were maids, especially when I saw their neat dresses.

I think religion was the strongest influence on the way we lived. In our village every family professed allegiance to either church or chapel. The superficial differences between the two were obvious. On the one hand was the lovely Norman village church, with its vaulted roof and stained glass windows, its robed clergy and surpliced choir, and the strict formality of its

Eyam church

ritual. On the other hand were the chapels with their starkly simple buildings and furnishings, the lusty congregation singing, the extempore prayers and informal services. We belonged to a chapel which even rejected paid ministers, relying instead on a panel of lay preachers drawn from largely untrained members of the community, whose fervour and sincerity outweighed any lack of scholarship.

Church attracted those who aspired to be gentry, or the type of poorer people who doffed their caps to the gentry! Its members were likely to vote Tory. The non-conformists were more egalitarian. The small trades people and workers, who were in the majority, had a strong Liberal tradition. (Socialists were rare and were suspected of being atheists.)

In spite of these differences the communities usually worked closely together. Weddings, funerals and christenings were always at the historic church, which everyone held in great affection. The whole village would unite to raise money to keep it in repair or to buy new bells or to extend the burial-ground. The various choirs would unite for special occasions, and harvest festivals and Good Friday services were attended by a cross-section of the community. Church organization like the Girls' Friendly Society welcomed young people of all denominations, as did the Band of Hope at chapel.

I find it strange that in the 1980s and 1990s we excuse crime and vandalism on the grounds of poverty. We were very poor, but most people upheld a high moral code. Whether we were 'church' or 'chapel' we studied the Bible and were taught reverence, truth, honesty and self-respect. Christian virtues included thrift, self-help and the passionate belief in our duty to help others even less fortunate than ourselves. In the absence of State schemes, even the poorest would help to raise money for voluntary organizations to help orphans, or the blind or hospitals. We even gave our pennies to support missionaries to take Christianity to far-off lands.

The duty to care for others showed most strongly in family life. It was unusual for mothers to go out to work, and children of working people were cared for at home until the age of five years. With large families and no labour-saving devices, looking after the home was a full-time job. Children were brought up to obey their parents, and to show respect to them and to all older people. In fact, the fifth commandment was held to be highly important through all stages of life. Many deprived families made great sacrifices to care for aged parents in their declining years. This spared them the humiliation of the lonely old folk who could only look forward to the dreaded workhouse, where they would be separated from husbands or wives, stripped of their meagre possessions, and left to wait for death.

At Sunday school they often talked to us about death. This was apt, as we were very familiar with death in the village, not only among the elderly, but all ages. Little babies died, perhaps from malnutrition or lack of medical care; some of our school friends died from measles, TB, scarlet fever, or other complaints no longer regarded as fatal; mothers died, often through self-neglect. I remember, as a child, being taken to pay my respects at the open coffin of a neighbour, and I even helped to carry the tiny coffin of a dead baby into church for its funeral.

Most deaths occurred at home. There were few of the hospital facilities we now take for granted, and it seemed natural and right to nurse members of the family and let them die in familiar surroundings, in the presence of those who loved them. There was usually a neighbour who would help with night-nursing, or care for children, and who, at the end, would lay out the body with loving respect. Death was surrounded by customs and rituals, the drawn blinds, the decent black clothes, the ceremonial visits of relatives and friends. Deep religious faith prevented this from being morbid. There was no shame in open grief, and this, together with the support of communal mourning, brought great emotional relief.

There still remained the problem of paying for a funeral when families were almost destitute. This was partially relieved by another self-help organization, the Penny and Halfpenny Burial Society. This had come into being in the late nineteenth century, as a response to the distressful infant mortality of the time. Most families paid either a penny or a halfpenny a week for every child or adult, and from the funds accumulated a grant was paid in the case of death. Some people also had tiny insurance policies, and

The Saxon cross in Eyam churchyard

I remember the importance given to these weekly payments, even when there was barely money for basic food.

One other example of family care was illustrated by the treatment of illegitimate children. There was a great deal of prudery, and births out of wedlock were considered a great scandal. There were financial as well as ethical reasons for this disapproval. On the other hand, it was rare in our village for an unmarried pregnant girl to be abandoned by her family. The actual birth was kept as secret as possible, but the child was usually accepted into the family, often passed off as the off-spring of the grandmother, or a married aunt. This led to confused relationships, but kept responsibility within the family (though they could ill afford an extra mouth to feed) and helped to protect the baby and its mother from ignominy.

These thoughts on the moral attitudes of my elders may seem rather morbid, but they are a reflection of my Wesleyan upbringing. I attended the little Wesleyan Reform Sunday school and chapel fifty yards down the lane from our cottage. There was a cheerful, almost jolly atmosphere. We often sang the most gloomy words to the liveliest melodies, as when we lustily sang the following words to the tune of 'Onward Christian Soldiers':

> Ye who teach the ignorant, help the sick and poor,
> Stand by when the enemy, Death is set at the door,
> Listen to the Master, for well-pleased is He,
> Those who help the poorest, do it unto Me.

Reference to death was a recurrent theme of our hymns, even when we were quite young. Each generation has its own inhibitions. In the 1990s we are no longer prudish about sex, but we shield our young from talk of death, and they are often only aware of it through fictional violence, or through tragic accidents. When I was young we were reticent about reproduction and the beginning of life, but we were familiar with death and accepted it quite openly.

I first went to Sunday School when I was four years old, joining a group of boys and girls ranging from toddlers to teenagers. Sunday was a busy day. We attended for an hour in the morning, and again for a session in the afternoon, after which all but the youngest were expected to stay on for the adult afternoon service. Those over the age of ten usually returned at six o'clock for the chapel evening service.

Older children helped the younger ones to find their way among the books of the Bible and to read aloud the chosen story for the week from both Old and New Testaments. There were texts to be learned, and often longer passages or Psalms. Some of the teachers had read the Bible from cover to cover, and they urged their charges to do likewise. One of the lasting effects was a love of the fine eloquent language of the authorized version.

There were other activities for members of the Sunday school. In summer there were outings and picnics. In winter there were mid-week club meetings and concerts (always advertised as 'Coffee and Buns') which needed weeks of rehearsals.

The chapel concerts were so called because of the refreshments provided in the interval – 'Camp' coffee and rock buns. The items performed were a strange mixture and were not necessarily of a religious nature. There might be ballads sung by talented bass or soprano soloists, piano or organ recitals, action songs by children from the Sunday school, humorous readings, recitations or violin solos. Some old faithfuls had party pieces, like old Sammy Sellars, postman and lay preacher, a wonderful old man, who had

Bakewell church

been declaiming 'The Burial of Moses' at every concert for twenty years. He had never been known to finish this lengthy poem, and as he got older his memory failed increasingly early in the saga, but no one minded, for after years of experience the whole audience were able to prompt him in unison whenever he stumbled, until he and everyone else collapsed in helpless laughter.

Then there were the special occasions celebrated by Sunday school and congregation together. The highlight was the Chapel Sunday School Anniversary, usually called 'The Sermons', which was usually held in the early summer. Additional seats were erected in a high tier facing the congregation, and there we children 'sat up', the girls wearing new hats and new dresses (probably their only new dress of the year) usually made for the occasion by fond mothers, and the boys with carefully combed hair, white shirts and neatly pressed jackets and shorts.

Below them sat the adult choir, the ladies mostly plump and corsetted, their crimped hair topped with straw hats ornate with flowers and ribbons. These were often prized purchases from the latest jumble sales. There were fewer men, but their fortissimo bass voices made up for any lack of musical art.

The local draper, J.T. Hancock, played the harmonium, twinkling through his steel-rimmed spectacles with great enjoyment. He was flanked by three or four ancient worthies playing fiddles, and a double bass, then came my father who had taught them the anthems, in proud control of us all as he wielded his baton.

Each year new hymns to new tunes were sung at the Sunday School Anniversary, and there was some rivalry between neighbouring villages, each anxious to present the best programme. The lyrics may have lacked poetic inspiration, but they were earnest and devout.

Hymn sheets were kept from year to year and I have a collection from my grandfather's time (1890–1900) when little children were taught to sing:

> Death, ere another year may strike
> Some in our number, mark'd to fall;
> By young and old prepared alike
> The warning is to each and all.

(Chorus)   Come happy children come and raise
> Your voice with one accord . . . etc

> Meanwhile our falling ranks renew
> Send teachers, children in our place;
> More humble, docile, faithful, true –
> More like THY Son – from race to race.

(See appendix two for further hymns from this period.)

As a child I found it hard to accept the insistence on being humble and docile. At day school we had to learn the Church of England catechism and were taught 'to do our duty in that state of life to which it had pleased God to call us'. I rejected this until I was adult then I realized that it should have read 'that state of life to which it *shall* please God to call me' so my rebellious attitude was not sinful after all!

By 1915 tastes were less morbid, and I remember singing:

> Jesus wants me for a sunbeam
> To shine for him each day
> In every way try to please him
> At work and school and play.

and

> Jesus bids us shine with a pure clean light,
> Like a little candle burning in the night,
> In this world is darkness, so we must shine
> You in your small corner, and I in mine!

Best of all we liked the offertory hymn:

> Hear the pennies dropping, listen while they fall,
> Every one for Jesus, He shall have them all!

Another important event in the year was the Harvest Festival. Again the tiers of staging were erected and covered with white sheets to make a large display stand for the offerings of fruit and marrows and home-made cakes and jams, vases of flowers and bowls of eggs. Children collected produce from local farmers, then built pyramids of potatoes, carrots and turnips in front of the altar rail. Swathes of oats and autumn flowers were tied round pillars and pew ends, cabbages, parsley and celery were stacked in the window sills and the edge of the gallery was festooned with asparagus fern and Chinese lanterns. The final touches were the bunch of black grapes, the harvest loaf and the glass jug of spring water on the white-clothed altar-table.

At the two services on Sunday we packed the pews, and amid the acrid tang of Chrysanthemums and the temptation of a profusion of apples, we loudly gave thanks that 'all is safely gathered in', though in that bleak district that was not always strictly true.

Christmas brought carol singing, and a few days later the 'chapel tea and prize-giving'. Three rows of trestle tables were arranged in the chapel and

The interior of Eyam church

the pews seats placed on either side. By the fire in the little boiler room we softened pound lumps of butter for the women making mountains of sandwiches, boiled ham for the adults and potted beef made by the local butcher for the Sunday school scholars. We drank vast quantities of tea and had mince pies and slices from a slab of bought fruit cake given by the village grocer. This was an unusual treat in those frugal times.

Then came a concert with plays, recitations and action songs by the children. The climax was the presentation of the coveted books which had been on display all evening. Every child had a prize, but they varied in value according to attendance. The stars of the evening were those who could boast 104 marks, having never missed a Sunday school session throughout the whole year.

Most of the children from the Sunday school went to the chapel in mid-week to the Band of Hope which was the juvenile section of the temperance movement. The members were children between the ages of about seven to fourteen. They were expected to sign the pledge, without really understanding what it meant. It was extremely unrealistic to encourage children to promise not to take alcohol for the rest of their lives. It was a nationwide organization, and with few other youth clubs to compete with, it had the sort of popularity later enjoyed by the Boy Scout and Girl Guide movements.

It is difficult to appreciate the depth of emotion aroused by the problem of alcohol in the late nineteenth and early twentieth century. My father and many thousands like him who worked for the Temperance Union and the United Kingdom Alliance sincerely believed that liquor was evil of itself, endangering the soul, ruining the health, and bringing poverty and squalor to the family. For over forty years there was persistent publicity for the temperance cause in the form of lectures, leaflets, books and magazines devoted to the subject (see appendix three).

The powers behind the movement were middle class, Liberal and Non-Conformist, and the avowed aim was to improve the plight of the poor. Obviously the attempt to persuade people to boycott strong drink was also an attack on the rich profits of the brewers and distillers.

The Puritan doctrine of rejecting the sinful and wasteful pleasures of this world was still strong in the chapels, and it was there that total abstinence was most fervently preached. Social conditions in our cities justified their concern. Shamefully low wages and frequent unemployment, with no relief or safeguards against poverty or illness, created miserable conditions in the slums, so it was no wonder men and women turned to drink. It was readily available and comparatively cheap (a pint of beer cost twopence in 1894).

Even at these prices the effect on family life could be disastrous. Wages were too low to buy even basic necessities and every penny spent on drink

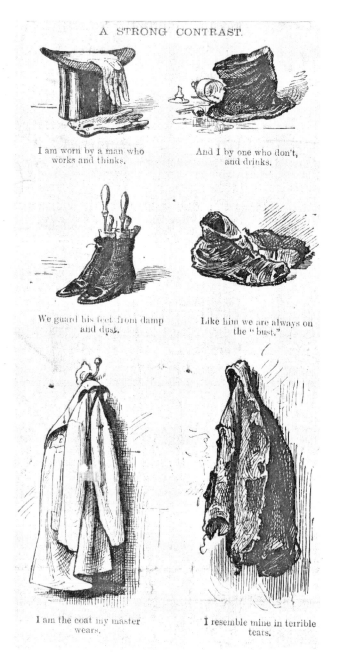

A STRONG CONTRAST.

I am worn by a man who works and thinks.

And I by one who don't, and drinks.

We guard his feet from damp and dust.

Like him we are always on the "bust."

I am the coat my master wears.

I resemble mine in terrible tears.

An illustration from *The British Workman*, deploring the abuse of alcohol

brought greater hardship. The habitual drinker was soon destitute, and since he was less efficient as a worker than a sober man he was in great danger of losing his job. No wonder the brewers were depicted in the same light as today's drug-pushers, as monsters getting rich on the degradation of the poor. Though drunkenness was not a major problem in villages like ours, the social conscience of the temperance workers was stirred by accounts of the plight of city dwellers living in squalor and poverty which went hand in hand with drunkenness. In such areas there would be as many as one public house to eight adult members of the population, ranging from the sordid gin-shops to the more pretentious beer palaces. There was little control in the nineteenth century on their numbers, or hours of opening or general conduct, and the enormous profits made by distillers and brewers rendered them a powerful vested interest.

The newly literate working class were showered with a torrent of temperance literature largely suggesting that if people lived in misery it was their own fault, and if they gave up drinking they could remedy the situation. Much of the propaganda was expressed in such extreme and melodramatic language that it must have defeated its own purpose.

It would be interesting to know who financed this steady stream of propaganda based on the theory that every man was master of his fate. It served to deflect attention from the greater scandal of starvation wages which were insufficient to provide the bare essentials of life, let alone stretch to afford innocent pleasure. It would seem to have been a disservice to social progress to lay the blame of a poverty-ridden lower class entirely on the unfortunate victims. It seems probable that behind the dedicated men of integrity who worked for the temperance cause there were influential groups whose motives were less pure.

But there was no doubt of the sincerity of the teetotallers I knew in my childhood. Two main considerations confirmed their beliefs. In the first place they set great store on the human dignity of every individual, and they feared the debasing effect of alcohol. This could lead to bigotry, like the refusal to allow drops of brandy to be given to a sick person when ordered by the doctor. Amusingly, the ban was rarely placed on home-made wine or beer, though that could be extremely potent. Secondly, they were fiercely determined to live decent lives with their families, and only by extreme thrift could this be achieved. However, we young Band of Hope members understood little of this.

My father was the leader of the Eyam branch of the Band of Hope which held mid-week meetings in the Wesleyan Reform Chapel. We had singing games and guessing competitions. Some of us learned little recitations or asked riddles, or tried to excel in a spelling bee. My father had a happy touch with children and we enjoyed ourselves immensely. He kept us spellbound with a new story every week, and we did not mind that it always had a moral. It might be about the evils of liquor, but more often it illustrated the lessons of honesty, truthfulness or kindness.

Two or three times during the summer we would have a Band of Hope picnic on a Saturday afternoon. Each with a bag of sandwiches and a tin mug, we would set off on the steep climb up Furness Wood and along the high road to Bretton. By the time we had scrambled down the rocky track to the bottom of the little valley of Breton Clough we were tired and hungry. Harry had by then had his white enamel bucket filled with clear water from the well of the nearest cottage, and two boys had managed to carry it to the picnic spot without spilling too much. Now came the great moment when a packet of lemonade crystals was stirred in, and we queued up to fill our mugs. We thought this was a marvellous drink. Afterwards the boys played cricket on the close turf, while the girls played 'hide-and-seek' or gathered heather and harebells and little herring bone ferns. My father knew every bird and every wild flower so that even the weary trudge home was full of interest.

Often we would stop at one of the many groups of hillocks of white fluor spa which occurred on the slops of Eyam Edge. We thought of the heaps as miniature mountains and valleys, rising about 10 ft high and providing a habitat for blue and yellow wild pansies, trefoils and tiny white alpine saxifrage. My father would explain that these were 'spoil heaps' from the lead-mines that had provided prosperity to the district the previous century. He would tell us stories of the miners and their strange customs.

For many centuries Eyam had been one of the richest lead-mining areas in England, and this accounted for the scars of excavation to be seen on the hillside. In its heyday it must have resembled the gold-rush regions of California. Few veins of lead were worked by rich mining companies, or even the land-owners. They were prospected by individuals or families who had taken advantage of the ancient and unique Derbyshire mineral rights which allowed anyone who wished to, to mine anywhere for lead (with a few exceptions) in the King's field, which is an area of about 150 square miles. The only restrictions were on churchyards, gardens and orchards. When the village school was built in 1877 three apple trees were planted in the playground, so that it could be designated an orchard. This effectively prevented spoil from the adjoining mine hillocks being dumped there. For hundreds of years lead-mining in Derbyshire was under the jurisdiction of the Great Barmote Courts, powerful and independent bodies which in some ways resembled the Stannery Courts which regulated tin-mining in Cornwall. These courts are of great antiquity, probably dating from the time of King John who first granted local mineral charters in this region.

Though now shorn of much of their power, the Barmote Courts still meet once or twice a year at Stoney Middleton and at Wirksworth. Under their chairman, the Bar-master, twenty-four 'jurymen' are sworn in to deal with disputes for the ensuing six months. Traditionally they share a meal of bread and cheese and beer, and smoke tobacco in long clay pipes provided for the occasion.

The mining laws superseded laws of trespass, and a miner could stake his claim anywhere he thought he could find lead. He did this by making his mark with a cross on the ground, and setting up his 'head-gear', a strong scaffold to carry winding gear to lift out buckets of earth and stone during his excavations. He then informed the Bar-master, who registered the claim. From that day the man had nine weeks to work his claim and produce lead. Every three weeks the Bar-master visited the site and made a nick in the upright post of the head-gear. (This had to be entirely of wood, with no iron bolts or nails.) At the end of the ninth week the Bar-master brought the official measuring dish. The original brass dish was made in 1509, and is still displayed in the Moot Hall at Wirksworth. It has a capacity of fourteen 'Wincester' pints, an old English standard measurement. The prospector had then to produce two dishes of lead ore, otherwise he forfeited his claim and anyone else could jump in and benefit from the work he had already done.

If the claim was successful the land-owner could not obstruct the miner in any way, but was compelled to allow him access to water and to a road, and enough land to tip the waste from the mine and to build an outbuilding. The new mine could bring riches or disappointment according to the thickness of the vein found or the difficulty of access. Underground water, and land-slides were frequent hazards, and tragedies were not unknown. No other mineral could be taken except lead ore, so the fluor spa and pyrites and limestone remained as man-made hills, which is why these hillocks are still a feature of the landscape.

During the eighteenth and nineteenth centuries the industry was very lucrative, and not only for the miners. Every thirteenth dish of ore was due to the lords of the mineral field. In 1895 these were the Duke of Devonshire, the Duke of Buckingham and Lord Hothfield. The rector of Eyam claimed his tithe, which was one penny for every dish of ore. Some idea of the prosperity may be seen by the fact that within a few years the rector's income increased from £50 per annum to over £1,000.

Disaster came for the miners towards the end of the nineteenth century. Underground streams seeped through the layers of limestone rock, and many mines were flooded. It was not economic to install efficient means of dealing with this. By 1900 most of the mines had been abandoned, and the men, formerly so independent, had to find whatever employment they could. Reminders of those times were still evident during my childhood. The 'Old Man', as the old lead-miner is still affectionately known, had left his mark, not only in his spoil-heaps and his rotting head-gear, but in deep shafts found unexpectedly on the rough hillside, and the marks of his pick in pot-holes and cave galleries. There were still lively memories of the lead-mining era. There were tales of fortunes won and lost, of dogged determination and of disasters, and of drinking and fighting in a tough community. Until 1914 there were still ten public houses in this small village, including the Miners Arms, and the Bull Ring, in front of which could still be seen the strong iron ring used when chaining the animals in the barbarous sports of bull- and bear-baiting.

CHAPTER SIX

What Did We Do In The Great War?

Keep the home fires burning,
Though our hearts are yearning,
Though the lads are far away,
they dream of home.
There's a silver lining,
Through the dark clouds shining,
Turn the dark clouds inside out
till the boys come home.

Popular wartime song

I was six years old when war broke out, and ten when the Armistice was signed. So I find it difficult to describe the effects of war on the village, as I cannot compare it with life in the pre-war years which I don't really remember. Shortage of money and of food and anxious regard to the news were to me just the normal conditions of life. All the younger men in the village were called up. Sometimes they returned on leave in khaki, or in naval uniform. Many were killed or posted as missing. My father was forty-four years old and partially deaf, so was not eligible for service. At some period the shoe factory was closed and he was directed to work in a steel-rolling mill in Sheffield, but he was back in his old job by the end of 1917, working for about half the national average wage.

My chief memory of him at that time is in his Home Guard uniform, going off for training on Salisbury Plain, or for local drill and target practice. His rifle always hung by his bed, and sometimes I would be allowed to help him clean it. He became a crack shot, as did several of his

Harold Froggatt, the first soldier
from Eyam to be killed in the
Great War

friends, and when war ended they decided to form a rifle club. Looking
back, I find it surprising that the authorities allowed them to keep their
rifles. The members constructed a rifle range up on the Edge road, with
butts at 25 and 50 yds. I often got the task of printing notices about
competitions and pinning them to the notice board. By then we had half a
dozen rifles hanging in the bedroom, and a good supply of ammunition in
boxes under the bed, for, of course, Harry took charge.

My second vivid memory of this time concerns Longshaw Lodge, a large
house 8 miles away, which had been taken over as a convalescent home for
wounded soldiers. I had been with my mother when she visited there in
connection with an article for the newspaper, and had been grief stricken

by the sight of these young men in their pale blue uniforms, with their crutches, bandaged eyes or amputated arms. I was seven or eight years old and I suppose this was my first experience of mutilation. I felt impelled to do something to help, so set myself up as a 'one child' collection service for comforts for wounded soldiers. Every Saturday morning till the end of the war I went begging to all the larger houses in the district, a round journey of a couple of miles. I would be given a teacake here, a couple of eggs there, or perhaps an orange or a few books. The driver of the station bus then took my offering to Grindleford station where it was picked up by a member of the hospital staff. Every week I had a personal letter from the matron thanking me in detail for the items. My mother kept these letters. Reading them now I am struck by the meagre contribution (no one had much to spare) and by the great insight of Sister Bull, who took a child's effort so seriously. Before the hospital closed I was fetched in a chauffeur driven car to have tea with 'my soldiers'.

Of course I was not the only member of my family who tried to help the war effort. My mother was on a committee whose object was to provide 'comforts' for local serving soldiers and sailors. She used to join a sewing party organized by one of the ladies of the village. They made warm shirts and were provided with khaki wool to knit balaclava helmets, mittens, scarves and socks. Then there was always the problem of money-raising. We helped national flag days for organizations such as the Red Cross, and Queen Alexandra's Nursing. To support local charities we made little posies of flowers from the cottage gardens, and sold them instead of flags.

As well as serving in the Home Guard my father organized events to raise money, usually by giving concerts with his concert party, The Eyam Variety Entertainers, which he had founded in 1911. They were a sort of rural amateur 'Black and White Minstrel Show', with their white suits and straw hats and faces blackened with burnt cork. There was a good deal of cross-talk patter and comic turns, as well as fine tenor and bass solos and choruses. They owed their repertoire largely to the music hall, choosing their items from catalogues of sheet music provided by a London theatrical firm. Few of the members ever had the opportunity to hear the items performed professionally, so their interpretations must have been highly individual.

This group of about twenty men looked to my father not only as their secretary but also as their leader. At Christmas they formed themselves into a carol party, starting up on the stroke of midnight of Christmas Eve outside our house, and continuing through the night to serenade the whole village to its farthest extremities, even to the outlying farms, where they were often regaled with wine or beer and mince pies in the early hours of the morning. This entailed my father being the victim of much good-hearted teasing about his teetotal principles.

The Longshaw Military Hospital
Wounded Soldiers' Comforts Fund (No. 66),

Registered under the provisions of Section 1 of the War Charities Act, 1916.

COMMITTEE :

C. DOLMAN,   A. J. WARD,
J. PROCTOR.   E. W. P. DOMICAN,
O. PATTERSON,   C. L. SUMPTER,
E. CARLISLE,   J. P. SPRY,
H. DEWHIRST,   T. O. FROGGATT.
    G. R. SLATER (Hon. Sec.),
    Telephone No. 1031 Central.

ROYAL INSURANCE BUILDINGS,

CHURCH ST., SHEFFIELD,

14th May   191

Dear Miss Dawson,

On behalf of Sister Keeton and my Committee I wish to thank you for the 20 eggs, 7 oranges and 8 books sent up to Longshaw last week.

Yours faithfully,

G. R. Slater

Miss Doris Dawson,
    Laurel Cottage,
        Eyam,
            Derbys.

A copy of a letter from the Longshaw Military Hospital, thanking Doris for her gift of food and books

The concert party sang traditional carols and some of purely local origin. Sometimes they included more ambitious anthems, like the florid 'Hail, smiling morn, that tops the hills with gold'. On one occasion when they had been celebrating rather freely they tackled this and only with difficulty managed the final flourish, 'Hail! Hail! Hail! Hail! Hail! Hail! Hail!, H-a-i-l, Hail!' losing most of the aspirates in the process. At this point a loud and somewhat tipsy voice added, 'There's plenty of "ale" about tonight, Harry!'

I have many memories of musical activities in those days. My father's pride and joy was his large Canadian organ, with a high Victorian super-structure of mirrors, shelves and carving, almost touching the ceiling. It had sixteen stops and two knee-swells, and could produce great beauty and variety of tone. As a young man Harry had managed to save up for this splendid instrument from his meagre wages. He was an extremly thrifty man, who neither smoked nor drank, and used to recall that his mother would proudly display the organ to her friends and refer to it as 'Harry's baccy money'. I remember him sitting for hours, lost in the music, as he played hymn tunes, parts of oratorios, melancholy folk songs or plantation tunes. His first tune was always 'Bonnie Mary of Argyll', which for some reason always moved him to tears.

He also had a violin and a flute, which I rarely heard, though he claimed that he could 'knock a tune out of anything'. He played plaintive tunes on his tin whistle, sometimes at home, but more frequently in the open air, sitting in the woods or on the rocks.

My mother had no musical talent, but she loved tunes and always sang while she worked. Her repertoire was quite different, and from her I learnt all the popular Edwardian ballads and music-hall songs. We would turn the mangle, or dolly the clothes in the wash-tub to the strains of 'Daisy', 'Lilly of Laguna', 'Waiting at the Church' or 'Comrades'. She had particular songs for different festivals. On St Stephen's Day she would strike up with:

> Hunt the wren says Robin the Bobbin,
> Hunt the wren, says Richard and Robin,
> Hunt the wren, says Jack o' the land,
> Hunt the wren, says everyone.

She needed little persuasion to proceed through all the verses, describing to me how groups of young men in the Isle of Man used to catch a wren and put it in a cage, then go from door to door singing this (like our Christmas carol singers, hoping for reward!). This naturally led to her airing her smattering of the Manx language, before singing 'Ellin Vannin' and the Manx Fisherman's hymn.

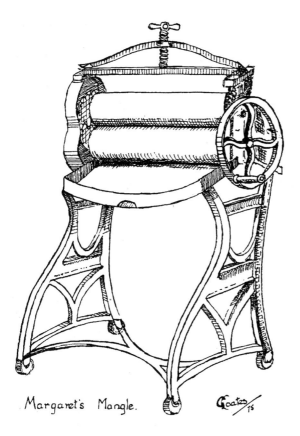

Margaret's Mangle.

On New Year's Eve a great log fire would blaze and before we children
went to bed she and my father sang the sentimental 'Miner's Dream of
Home' in which we joined in the chorus:

> I saw the old homestead and faces I loved,
> I saw England's valleys and dells,
> I listened with joy as I did when a boy
> To the sound of the village bells,
> The lamp was burning brightly,
> 'Twas a night that would banish all sin
> For the bells were ringing the Old Year out
> And the New Year in.

Friends often came in to sing to Harry's accompaniment. It might be
some of the chapel choir, or members of the Variety Entertainers trying out

new numbers, or just a random group of us harmonizing in an impromptu sing-song.

It was through wartime conditions that my mother found a way to augment our family income by a very small amount, and, incidentally, to make new friends. During that time seaside holidays were impossible, so many people in Sheffield sought brief recreation in walks over the moors on Sundays, or a few days in the country. In common with several other cottages, my parents put up a board advertising 'Hot water and teas'. During the worst of the rationing it was common for walkers to carry not only their sandwiches, but also a can or jug with tea and sugar in a screw of paper. They would pay mother with a copper to provide boiling water to brew the tea, and to add milk. Sometimes people called asking for food, and when supplies made it possible we would provide a 'plain tea' of home-made bread and butter and home-made jam, and perhaps a piece of cake for 6d. Sometimes it was possible to obtain eggs, and then boiled eggs were served in addition to the bread and jam, and the princely sum of 9d. per person would be charged. These meals were served at the family table, or in the garden on warmer days. I doubt whether there was much profit in this enterprise, but callers became 'regulars' and many long-lasting friendships began.

Sometimes people would ask if we could 'put them up' for a few days – some old friends of long standing, some who had got to know mother through 'her teas'. We hadn't much room, but a 'chairbed' downstairs for me would leave my bedroom vacant for a couple. They had to bring their own rations during the war, of course, but mother cooked and waited on them, and charmed them, I think. As for dad, he was never happier than when he could conduct visitors to historic sites or beauty spots, and his knowledge and tales were in much demand. Again, it wasn't a money-spinner. I think they charged about 2s. a day, but it eked out the housekeeping costs.

One frequent visitor, who often stayed for several weeks at a time, was a Miss Shemald, who had been a friend of my parents for many years. We children always called her Aunty Sally. She was in her late eighties and lame, but sprightly for all that. She would walk every day the half mile to the spring and water trough on the Grindleford road, to sample the pure water. I still possess the little Crown Derby mug she always carried in her handbag for the purpose. I think she had a tiny private income, but mother only let her pay 10s. a week, and in return she helped with the sewing and ironing.

I don't think my mother was very robust, but I remember her bringing energy and enthusiasm to all she did, whether it was walking from village to village to collect news items for my father to write up reports, or organizing her friends and neighbours in self-help efforts or working in the farmer's field.

I have mentioned that our small farmers relied on casual unpaid labour, and we were one of the families involved. All the family were expected to help, and on summer evenings and Saturday afternoons and at holiday times I accompanied my parents, with my young brother, who was a delicate child, strapped in his push-chair and left in the shade of the usual Derbyshire stone wall. In spring we would set potatoes, following the manure cart, and pressing in the potatoes about 18 in apart, working to keep ahead of the horse-drawn plough which followed to close the furrows. The children had to keep the baskets of seed potatoes replenished from sacks strategically placed around the field.

I remember one occasion when I was very young, and we were setting potatoes in a field high up at the edge of the moors. I struggled with my basket towards the wall, and was terrified when a harsh voice shouted, 'Go back, go back, go back'. I dropped my potatoes and ran to my father in great distress. It took some time to convince me that all I had heard was a bird, a grouse making his territorial call.

Then we would help in the hayfield, raking, tedding, then piling it into haycocks. This might have to be done several times if we were not blessed with good weather, but eventually the hay would be dried and we would have the excitement of riding on top of the load as it was carted to the barn or haystack.

Most years there was an odd field of oats and we would follow the horse-drawn reaper and gather up armfuls and tie it with twisted straw to make sheaves. These sheaves were made into stooks, each of six sheaves with the cut stalks on the ground and the ears leaning together in an inverted V shape. These were stacked when dry to be threshed later. Harvest tended to be late in the Peak, so that it was frequently spoiled by heavy rain, and might even remain in the field till it was mildewed and a total loss.

Our final effort of the season was potato-picking. The machine spun them out of the peaty soil and we gathered them in large baskets which we repeatedly emptied into sacks at the end of each row. We made sure that every potato was picked up, and anxiously counted the number of sacks produced by each row. Only when the whole field was cleared would we know what our reward was for our help throughout the season. Usually it was two or three hundredweights of potatoes which would be a valuable part of our food supplies for the winter.

At this time my mother initiated a community effort which was to be of lasting benefit to the village. She had always been concerned about the great hardship endured by families when they were stricken by sickness or accidents. The expense of medical treatment added to their worries, and no other help was available, except from kindly neighbours. She had read of district nursing associations which were being introduced in some parts of

The Nursing Association in August 1943 in honour of Nurse Perrin's twenty-five years at Eyam. Margaret Dawson is third from the right, standing behind the young man who was the first baby delivered by the nurse in 1918

the country, and was convinced that what we needed was a village nurse. This was a scheme without national funding, so each community was responsible for the payment of its own nurse's expenses. Mother arranged a meeting of a few of her friends to discuss the possibility. They decided that if every family in the village could be persuaded to contribute a few coppers a week they might be able to raise enough money to make a start. A public appeal was made, and a team of convassers trudged round the village enrolling members, and the Eyam Nursing Association was formed. The members were determined that its organization should be run at grass roots level but it was obvious that greater funding was necessary. They decided to ask for subscriptions from the more affluent members of the community. These were not the factory bosses, but people thought of as 'the gentry'. Some had business interests in Sheffield, and lived in large houses in the village. Some occupied a couple of local halls, living on inherited wealth. There was even one pianist of international renown who lived with his wife in a lovely house near the dell. Of course it was mother who went to see the 'ladies from the big houses'. Many of her friends would have held them in awe, but she had a happy facility of ignoring social class, as well as great eloquence in advocating her cause.

Mother not only succeeded in getting financial help, but found people willing to deal with the various officials who would need to be involved. One benefactor even presented a cottage for use as the nurse's residence. There were money-raising events, like whist-drives and soon they were able to buy furniture, and a nurse's bicycle. So it was that in August 1917 Nurse Perrin the district nurse and midwife arrived. For a generation she was to minister to the needs of us all, from the cradle to the deathbed. I still treasure a photograph of Nurse Perrin and the original members of the nursing association committee who were still running it on its twenty-fifth anniversary.

CHAPTER SEVEN

No Power To The Workers

But I don't allow it's luck and all a toss
There's no such thing as being starred and crossed.
It's just the power of some to be a boss,
And the bally power of others to be bossed.

Anon., about 1912

So it was that our district nurse arrived in 1917, a crucial time in the life of the village. Self-help and thrift had done something to ameliorate life's perpetual difficulties, but with wartime strains, long working hours and wages in the factories barely half the national average, morale was low. When the suggestion was made that workers should join a union and fight for their rights, some were apathetic, while others saw this as the only hope of improving their conditions.

Trade unions had strengthened during the war, when there was a great demand for labour to fulfil Government contracts. The National Union of Boot and Shoe Operatives (NUBSO) had achieved good conditions for workers in Northampton, Leicester and other large centres. A working week of forty-eight hours was agreed, and with wage increases and bonuses it was possible to earn 45–55s a week (£2.25–£2.75).

By 1917 the union was turning its attention to smaller centres. John Buckle was appointed organizer to recruit members in Eyam and Stoney Middleton, and to try to bring conditions in the factories up to union standards. He met with obdurate resistance from the bosses. Any worker who was suspected of joining the union was sacked instantly.

Seven firms were involved in the dispute. Four, in Stoney Middleton, all made heavy boots for men, pit boots, army boots and carters' boots. Three factories in Eyam manufactured light shoes for women and children. They were all family firms, and the bosses were what was known as 'little masters' who came from the same background as most of their employees, and spoke with the same Derbyshire accent. They had no pretence to culture or education, and treated with suspicion people like my parents who were well-read (though self-educated) and who were not afraid to express their opinions.

Of course as a child I did not understand all that was happening, but I have been able to study John Buckle's reports to union headquarters, by courtesy of NUBSO. The following quotations show the strength of the opposition he faced:

Mon. Dec. 1st 1917.
I visited Eyam to take up my duties with a view to organising. Several meetings arranged, both open air and indoors.

Jan. 1st 1918.
Open air meeting in the dinner hour. Well attended. Operatives appeared somewhat interested. Arranged further meeting at 'The Bull' at night. Good business. Eyam Branch formed with 43 members (all male).

Jan. 2nd 1918.
Open air meeting at Stoney Middleton. Well attended but no results for union, although village parson (Rev. Riddlesdon) says I made a good impression. At night met Eyam Branch – talk on what Union stood for.

Jan. 3rd 1918.
Organizing meeting of females at Bull's head, Eyam. Well attended. 46 female members made. They work 59 hrs week, no bonus paid, and wages very near the bone. The worst I have seen. Can something be done for them? God help them all. This surely is another 'Eyam Plague of the 17th Century'. The plague this time being long hours and small wages.

Jan. 4th 1918.
Open Air meeting at Stoney Middleton. Good attendance. Keen interest. No members! Operatives work 58½ hours week with no bonuses whatsoever.

Jan. 5th 1918.
Further meeting in Eyam, again going well. In afternoon entered up book for Eyam secretary and dealt with cards and minutes. (Sec. Bill

Slater). Then went to meeting at Stoney Middleton. Good meeting assembled, but landlord said 'no' so I hope to arrange a meeting for another night. (still hope in snows of the Peak District.)

Jan. 6th 1918.
Dinner hour meeting at Stoney Middleton. No members. (Intimidation?)

Jan. 9th 1918.
Metting at Stoney Middleton in reading room. 21 males joined the union. Male operatives are making pit boots, carter's boots, navvies' boots, 9 pairs per day for 35/- per week for 58½ hours.

Jan. 10th 1918.
Met Stoney Middleton & Eyam members at night. Decide not to have separate branch for Stoney Middleton.

Jan. 11th 1918.
Meeting of female operatives at Stoney Middleton. Highest wage 16/- a week of 55½ hrs. No war bonuses paid.

Jan. 12th 1918.
I regret to say this day Mr Slater, the Eyam Branch Secretary, got a weeks notice, the employer saying he would have no dictation from the union. So, the courageous secretary has to go, perhaps from his native village because he dared to take up the branch Secretaryship. His

Demonstration in Eyam, March 1918, outside the doctor's house. Harry Dawson stands in a cloth cap left of the bowler-hatted union official

employers are Ridgeways Bros. who impose a 59 hour week, with no war bonuses.

Jan. 15th 1918.
I have gathered information that employers are not going to ask for exemption for men of military age because they have joined the union. What a business. While a man is outside the Union the employer appeals on the ground of his indispensability to his business, and gets it on that count. When same man joins the Union he is no longer necessary.

Jan. 18th 1918.
Stoney Middleton. Dinner hour meeting. I had a conversation with one of the employers, who said, 'All men must go into the Army. I shall not claim any further exemption for them'. He also accused the union of trying to take all work away from country places. This firm once had a contract for army boots!

Jan. 18th 1918.
(Evening) meeting of Eyam Committee. There was indignation about the Branch Secretary's discharge, and members wanted to cease work. I told them to leave it in the hands of the Council of the Unions. Bill Slater is to be employed by the union, visiting house to house in the district at no less wages than he would have received in the factory.

(Same date).
Mr Tom Barber (Branch President) sacked by E. West and Son who got information from a little girl! *Also* four more men sacked by Ridgeway Bros.

One of these was Henry Dawson, my father, who was sacked on suspicion. Actually he hadn't joined the union in that first fortnight, cautiously waiting to see if it was likely to be effectual. Of course he soon became a member (see p. 84).

The following notes are taken from the monthly report of the General Council of the union, reported by E.L. Poulson, secretary of the union.

Feb. 1918.
Eyam. On Feb. 4th at Councils request we all went to Eyam with the intention of inviting them to pay to our National Conditions. The object of our visit Trade Unionism, had always been taboo. In 1912 five persons had been suspended for 10 days because they were suspected of joining a Union. Mr Buckle's formation of a union branch has been successful:- there are 80 members, plus Secretary, President and Committee.

At the end of the first week the Secretary was discharged. At the end of the second week the President, one committee member and 3 others were discharged. Tried to see the employers, but all refused point blank, saying 'We want nowt to do wi the Union'.

Feb. 17th.
The Council has sought the intervention of the Minister of Labour. (In Eyam operatives work 59 hours for 22–26/- per week.)

Mr J. Buckle's report continues:

Thurs. Feb. 21st.
Branch Meeting. Told them the council desired them to hand in their notices with the view of fighting the situation on hours and bonuses. Committee agreed to hand in notices on Feb. 28th (Eyam) and March 1st (Stoney Middleton).

Visit to Eyam of Mr W. Boden, Secretary of the National Gas Workers Union.

Feb. 23rd.
Went to Bakewell Tribunal to appeal for 10 operatives who firms refused to appeal for. Temporary exemption for one month granted.

Feb. 25th.
Notices handed in. Meetings continue.

· *Letter sent to Will Thorne, MP* asking him to ask a question in the house of Commons on Bakewell Tribunal Proceedings.

The strike called on 28 February 1918 was to drag on for two years before it fizzled out without achieving the object of union recognition. Reports during this period are naturally sporadic; the following again come from John Buckle:

May 26th–27th 1918.
Negotiating with Heginbottom and Sons at Stoney Middleton. The firm has orders for war-time boots and has the leather to start, but no boots have been made for 6 weeks owing to the strike. I have told him that he will not make a boot in 1918 unless he starts under the National Agreement Conditions and sticks fast to them. *Not* as he did with his previous contract for Russian boots (army order) to pay

Labour parade, Stoney Middleton, 22 April 1918

minimum wages during production of order, and then revert to 49 hours and bad wages.

The firm of Lennon & Mason have sold up their business. J.H. Thomas, MP has been asked to instruct Railway Union Members not to handle goods at Grindleford station. *No co-operation.*

Sunday a.m. (same week).
There was a joint Labour and Union Church Parade at Stoney Middleton. The Vicar, the Rev. J.B. Riddlesden preached a service on the text, 'Am I my brother's keeper?'.

Because the vicar allowed this service no one attended his church on Sunday evening. The parade was a large gathering and included J.J. Limb, representative of Sheffield Munition Workers and Wm. Boden (National Gas Works Organizer). Buckle says a 'military band' was in attendance. (This was actually Eyam Village Brass Band – see picture above.)

Minutes – June 23rd, 24th, 1918.

General Secretary, E.L. Poulson:
I went to Eyam on Saturday June 1st. I had a meeting with the employers but failed to reach agreement.
I had interview with Wm Nixon Esq. J.P. of Eyam whose help and influence was promised in approaching employers with a view to arbitration.

Will Thorne, MP, addressing strikers in Eyam Town End, summer 1918

Mr J. Buckle reported that he had settled with the firm of Heginbottom. He understood that 3 other firms were making only 3 doz. pairs a week, and he believed the strike could be brought to an end if an independent person was brought in.

W.M. Thorne, MP has visited the district on two occasons and addressed meetings.

From J. Buckle's later reports:

July 29th 1918.
The efforts of W M Nixon Esq., have failed and the employers still refuse to recognise the union.

Oct. 27th.
The strikers are determined on Union recognition, although the employers are offering better wages.

The problem of the dispute was raised in Parliament by W.M. Thorne, MP (see appendix four). From this date monthly meetings are reported, but no progress was made.

Dec. 27th 1918.
Employers still refuse. The influenza epidemic has hit this district, and two female members have died.

Jan. 27th 1919.
Visited Eyam, and together with Eyam secretary, Bill Slater, met the employers, who again said they would submit to no union interference.

At the last Branch meeting Mr J.J. Limb, rep. Munitions workers of Sheffield, was present. He presented £30 collected by munition works to the dispute fund.

Sat. March 15th 1919.
A labour demonstration was held in the open air, followed by a social in the evening which raised £11 for Eyam Nursing Association Fund. J.J. Limb presented £20 to strike fund from Sheffield munition workers.

General Council Meeting. 26th May 1919.
Mr J. Buckle was empowered to obtain a piece of land central to Eyam on which to build a factory to employ female members still on strike, and so to take them off strike pay. The finance to be organised by Mr Buckle and Union colleagues.

June 26th 1919.
The above being proceeded with.

Aug. 25th.
Army hut purchased.

Finally, from Buckle's report of December 1919:

I have visited Eyam and Stoney Middleton during the month. The position at Eyam is the same, but at Stoney Middleton it has changed owing to the attitude of Heginbotham who had previously settled. He is paying operatives £2.7s. for 50 hours. Non union employers are now paying day-work £2.10s for 50 hours. This has brought into existence the feeling that he is not playing the game, and on investigation I find that he is finishing goods for smaller employers. He is determined to assist them to ignore the Union, I have said we have no intention of a further strike at Stoney Middleton in view of the fact that we have reduced hours from 59 to 50 per week, and raised wages from 22 shillings to 47 shillings and 50 shillings per week.

We are relying on a Government Bill to make law a 48 hour week and a minimum rate of wages agreed by the Association of Employers and Workmens Union.

The union (Boot and Shoe Operatives) which could function successfully in towns like Northampton, was completely ineffectual in this rural dispute. In 1920 the president had to admit:

Eyam and Stoney Middleton strikers parade near the Lover's Leap Inn, Stoney Middleton. Harry Dawson is standing alone in front of the parade (extreme left). The tall man in a dark suit and trilby is John Buckle, the union organizer.

Eyam we have fought for over two years and are still fighting. My friend Buckle felt that if we had had the help of the railwaymen in the beginning we would have won.

Everything we could invent we have tried, but without success, in forcing the firms to accept our conditions. These people are asking for that kind of liberty rampant in Adam's time – the right of joining a trade union.

It is interesting to note that by the end of the first six months the union had paid out strike pay at Eyam to the sum of £1,566, out of a national total of £1,589. A note in a monthly report dated 23 August 1920 states that the strike had been the longest in the union's forty-six year existence, and had cost £8,445 1s. 6d.

It is remarkable that such a large proportion of the working people of the village should have the courage to continue the struggle for two years. They were an unlikely bunch of militants, men like Farewell Barnes, and Little Alan Slater, Tommy Barber, the irrepressible comic turn of the Variety Entertainers, the women and girls from the candle-lit machine room, the clickers, the finishers and the boys from buffing machines.

They were doomed to failure. Looking back seventy years from today's social conditions it is hard to realize how vulnerable these people and their families were. There was no free national health service, no unemployment pay (except a non-contributory scheme for engineering building and ship-building workers), no old-age pension until the age of seventy, when Lloyd George's famous 5s. (25p) a week was paid; no family allowance. People could be sacked from their jobs or evicted from their homes without redress, and since the employers could bring undue influence to bear on trades people and officials, the threat of victimization hung over everyone.

Hunger and fear drove a few men back to work. The offer of some extra payments tempted others. (Bribery sometimes took odd forms. I was recently told of an instance by an old gentleman who was a schoolboy at the time, living close to one of the shoe factories. He told me of the fish-cart which stopped by his house, and the boss who appeared to carry away a box of herrings each week as a reward for the 'blacklegs'.)

For the rest of the strikers there was little help. They held their rallies and their marches and had visits of union leaders and depended on their self-help organizations – the friendly society, the burial club, and the newly-formed nursing association.

It must not be thought that the strike, or even the struggle for existence, occupied all our thoughts. The war was still raging on the Marne and Somme, boats were sinking allied shipping, rationing became even more severe. There were frequent telegrams to wives and mothers reporting husbands or sons 'missing presumed dead'. Soldiers were being repatriated, gravely wounded. This last year of the war, and the following months were steeped in misery which crushed even the most optimistic spirits.

On a lighter note this led to my parents being involved in social activities to raise the money for 'soldiers' comfort funds'. The Eyam Variety Entertainers had to be rehearsed for concerts, there were flag days, and socials.

I was nearly ten years old in mid-January when my father came home with the news that he had been sacked from his job. My parents reacted to the shock with anger, and with tears. Others who had been dismissed had become members of the union, but my father had not yet joined, and was merely sacked on suspicion. There would be a pay day at the end of the week in which he worked his notice, but after that there would be no income at all. at that time there was no unemployment pay. (The 1911 unemployment scheme was limited to three trades: building, engineering and shipbuilding, where work patterns fluctuated. It covered about 3 million workers.) My father wasn't a member of the union, and it was to be another six weeks before a strike was called, so there was no strike pay either.

Up to that time we were poor because the wages were barely half the national average. Now we were practically destitute. We were too proud to ask for Poor Relief, and on no account would either of my parents run up debts. There were a few shillings a week for the local reports in the *Derbyshire Courier* (at 1d. a line I don't suppose it amounted to much). There was no casual work in Derbyshire in January. My father would mend neighbours' shoes for a few coppers, and my mother vainly trudged round some of the bigger houses trying to get domestic work. I remember that she went to Farnley Farm to do some wallpapering. This meant a walk of about 3 miles each way – down Eyam Dale, to the right along Middleton Dale to the Cupolo Quarries, and up a long unmade lane to the farm. She came home delighted to have received ½ lb of butter as well as being paid for her work. I earned a few coppers running errands, delivering weekly newspapers, pushing babies out in their prams, or fetching pails of water from the village square. Neighbours had little enough money for themselves but usually found me some job as an excuse to give me a penny or a halfpenny. Somehow we scraped together enough to buy flour and the meagre wartime ration of tea and sugar. But each day brought the fear of hunger. From the butcher mother got a 'pennorth' of bones, and a bit of suet to render down for dripping on our bread. We had soup every day. Fortunately we had our winter store of potatoes and some of the previous autumns's jam. We couldn't afford our usual milk, but it was possible to buy skimmed milk for ½d. a quart from Dr Brookes, who kept dairy cattle, and made his own butter. So I did a daily walk after school carrying the milk in a china jug, and hoping I wouldn't meet any rough boys who would jostle me.

My father had plenty of time to collect firewood from the woods so we always had a fire, but paraffin cost money, and we sometimes had to make do with candles, which we lit with spills made from old letters or newspapers.

My mother was adept at running a household on very little money, but even she had never faced such frightening penury as we suffered in those first few months of 1918. We had had short periods without money before, as no holidays were ever paid for, and the factories always closed down for a week in late August, and for bank holidays. But on those occasions we had saved up previously to bide us over. Now my parents were at their wits end, not only to provide food, but to pay the rent. Although several generations of my father's family had lived in the cottage, they did not own it. Failure to pay rent could cause immediate eviction – there was no protection. By the second week in March those operatives who had joined the union came out on strike. This was about four-fifth's of the work force. Those who remained at work were motivated more by fear than loyalty. Some had large families, some were expecting 'call up papers' (conscription was for men between eighteen and forty-one years) and some were afraid to lose their homes. Many of the cottages were owned by employers who threatened eviction to men who joined the union. Rideway Bros continued some production, but very little. Wives, daughters and other female relatives of the bosses who had never worked before, were brought in to work the sewing machines. Money inducements were offered to people with no experience of shoe-making. Later in the year when soldiers were being demobilized, some were tempted to go in and help. There was great bitterness in the community and for the first time I heard the epithets 'scabs' and 'blackleg'.

Even when the strike became official, my father's position was still awkward. He was not a union member, and not 'on strike' as he had been dismissed previously, so he didn't qualify for payment from the union. Eventually John Buckle and some of the committee came to see him, saying they needed him; he joined the union, and after some time I think they awarded him strike pay, as things at home got slightly better.

Family harmony had been strained during those months. My mother was convinced that dad had secret savings which he could have used to relieve our hardship. He angrily denied it. (Actually he had a small amount of money saved but was fearful of using this in case some even worse disaster should happen, and we should have to go to the workhouse – this was a constant dread.)

Once father became involved in the union he brought to it the same 'drive' that marked all his activities. He was soon organizing pubic meetings and parades, involving the local band, speaking on out-door platforms, marshalling marchers. Our home became a centre of activity. John Buckle was a regular caller, and visiting speakers were always brought to the cottage, sure of mother's welcome and a cup of tea. So we often saw J.J. Limb the Gasworkers' Union secretary and William Boden of the Munition Workers, and even had a brief visit from the great Will Thorne (see appendix four).

My father's former bosses were furious and sent a message saying that not only would they never employ him again, but they would make sure that no other employer in the village would give him a job. So we seemed doomed to scrape an existence on about £1 a week.

The official union reports already quoted (see pp. 74–81) explain the next two years better than my childish memories. It is a story of the working people of that period, and the powerlessness of a small union to help them.

The summer of 1918 came, and surprisingly my father found himself in work for a few months. When war broke out he was forty-four years old – too old for compulsory military service. When in the middle of 1918 the age for conscription was raised to fifty he received his call-up papers. When he attended for medical examination he was declared unfit for military service owing to deafness, and was directed to war work. I think it would be August when he was ordered to report to a steel-rolling mill in Sheffield as a labourer. Some munition workers had been getting high wages, but this was one of the less well-paid jobs. Daily transport was impossible in those days so it meant paying for lodgings in Sheffield all week, with fares home at the weekend, which took a good slice of his wages, but at least for a short time there was some security. So, the war continued, and the strike continued. More reports came of local boys killed in action. There were few young men in the village, and the older men, women and girls were without work.

At last 11 November came, and news of the Armistice. There was more stunned disbelief than jubilation. In any case, what did it signify? Would it really be 'Peace' or just a lull before further conflict? We didn't really understand. The church bells rang, and there was a service of Thanksgiving Prayers. It was not until the following year, after the treaty signed by the Germans on 28 June at the Palace of Versailles that a day was set aside nationally to celebrate the end of the war. I remember a big open-air concert in Eyam, on the green opposite the hall, with a band, some well-known vocalists, and a choir assembled from churches and chapels in Eyam and Foolow, conducted by my father in choruses from 'Messiah', including, of course, the 'Hallelujah Chorus'.

On 11 November, however, we also had cause to grieve, as news came to the cottage of my friend, Mary Hawkesworth, to say that her eighteen-year-old brother, Private Henry Hawkesworth, had died in hospital – a last minute victim of war.

Now changes came quickly. By 14 November it was announced that an election would take place on 14 December. So by the end of December my father, and countless other 'war workers' were dismissed from their jobs. By Christmas 1918, we had two good things to be thankful for – the relief of the end of the war on 11 November, and the elation of getting our Liberal candidate into Parliament early in December (see Chapter Eight).

However, on the whole, the first winter after the Armistice was a time of great misery, not only for our village, but for the whole of the country. In his book, *Britain Between the Wars–1918–1940*, C.L. Mowat wrote:

The first winter of peace brought little comfort. There was a serious shortage of coal. We sat shivering around very small fires, and the shadow of the great influenza epidemic darkened many a doorstep.

It had first reached England in June 1918 and gradually increased in severity, until in the worst week in early November, 7,560 persons died of influenza in London and 96 other large towns. The epidemic then declined, but a new outbreak began late in January 1919 and reached its peak at the beginning of March, when 3,889 deaths were recorded in London and the other 96 towns. A survey made in Manchester showed that half the people contracted it, and 7.9% succumbed to it. The 'flu respected neither youth nor age, but was mostly deadly to children under one, of whom 2.2% died of it. In England and Wales as a whole 150,000 persons died of influenza, gleaner of war's harvest.

(*Britain Between the Wars – 1918–1940*, C.L. Mowat, London, 1955. Reproduced by permission of Metheun and Co.)

By December the flu epidemic was rife in Eyam, and several friends had died. My father was without work again, so we had no regular income. It was to be another year before a system of unemployment pay was instituted for people in his plight. The strike was still dragging on, and the winter was severe. We were managing somehow, but another blow was in store.

It was towards the end of the Christmas holidays and I had got the job of 'baby-minding' for a Mrs Daniels who kept a bakers and grocery shop in the square (I was ten years old remember). I had just wheeled little Beatrice's pram into the house, when I fell down in a faint. It was just time for the village bus, and they were able to stop it in the square, and get George Marples to drive me home. They put me on the sofa, and by night

The stocks and doctor's house, Eyam

time I was in a fever and delirious. Aunty Sally was staying, and she and mother took turns to sit by me.

As if that was not enough, the next day my father returned from tramping around the farms looking for work, with his face swollen and ulcerated, and he too was quite ill. Of course we sent for Dr Brookes – a rough character with no bedside manner. He examined me first and said I had double pneumonia, and would probably not survive. (I was to learn later that the lady I had been working for, and Eliza Willis who worked in the shop, both died of 'flu within a few days. They had been buried before I recovered.)

The doctor then saw my father, and diagnosed anthrax, and said he was to go to an isolation hospital. When my mother asked what chance there was of recovering from that disease, he said, 'None'. Poor mother! She said if there was no treatment and he must die, she would nurse him at home till the end. So we had a nightmare time, though it was a while before I was fully conscious of what was happening. Aunt Sally nursed me downstairs by the fire, applying thermogene instead of the prescribed linseed poultice. Mother spent most of her time keeping dad comfortable and bathing his poor face. Somehow my brother George got cared for. Needless to say I recovered, but it was a long time before I was strong again – a legacy, no doubt, of poor wartime rations and poor diet because of poverty.

As for my father, when he had survived for over a week, Dr Brookes decided it couldn't have been anthrax, but evidently was 'erysipelas', a virulent form of eczema. One can imagine the agony my mother must have suffered in those weeks.

Charlie White's campaign leaflet for the 1910 elections

CHAPTER EIGHT

People's Champion

I always think it comical
How nature always does contrive
That every boy and every gal
That's born into the world alive
Is either a little Liberal
Or else a little Conservative!

Sir W.H. Gilbert, 'Iolanthe'

In the face of all our difficulties our family remained stubbornly optimistic. My parents were not content with 'that state of life to which it had pleased God to call them'. We had visions of a fairer life, and the conviction that we could improve life by our own efforts. Politics and education seemed to offer some hope, and against all the odds we struggled in both fields during those troubled years, 1918–22.

I have already mentioned that while Eyam was suffering the poverty and depression caused by the strike, two dramatic national events had a considerable impact on our lives. The first, of course, was the signing of the Armistice on 11 November 1918, and the knowledge that no more local men would be killed, and those serving in the forces would come home. Following this, on 14 November, it was announced that there was to be a General Election

All my childhood I had been accustomed to hearing my father and his friends discussing politics. They encouraged me to make yellow rosettes and paste yellow posters on notice-boards with messy flour paste. They were all dedicated Liberals of course. Though up to that time my mother had no vote, she was as devoted as my father was to the cause, and just as violently opposed to Toryism. Two names mentioned with a touch of reverence in our home were Lloyd George and Charles White, the Liberal candidate. Only from them could we expect care for the old, the poor, or the war widows. They were thought of as the natural champions of our class. Not that all working-class men were Liberals. The Nonconformists were solidly loyal, as were most small shopkeepers and craftsmen. But the so-called gentry, and in a feudal way, the people who worked for them, and many Church of England members, usually voted Tory. There was snobbishness involved. Liberals were 'little men', while Tories were represented by the Duke of Devonshire and his family (the Cavendishes) on his great estate at Chatsworth.

The Labour Party did exist, of course, but in spite of Labour parades in support of the strike, they made no impact on the community, and there was no Labour candidate. (My father thought the socialists were 'wild men' and derided their ideas on the redistribution of wealth. He felt that the hard working and thrifty would suffer, while the spendthrifts and shiftless would reap rewards they didn't earn. It was Puritanical conviction.) 'Charlie' White, as he was affectionately known, had been admired by my father and his friends for many years. He was a poor man, who had dedicated his life to the service of the community. He was born in 1860 at Tetbury in Gloucestershire, and moved to Derbyshire in about 1880. He lived at Bonsal where he started a cobbling business. His great interest in public affairs led him into politics, and he eventually became chairman of Matlock District Council. During his term of office much improvement and modenization was carried out in the town, including the building of the Grand Pavilion. In the local Liberal movement he worked his way to the top by sheer force of will, until he became election agent for the then Liberal candidate, a Mr Himmers.

Charles White himself was first adopted as candidate in 1910. He knew that he was unlikely to be elected in this strong Tory constituency (West Derbyshire), but he acquired a network of loyal workers in most of the villages who dreamed of eventually being strong enough to fight the Cavendish family who regarded the seat as theirs by right.

The outbreak of war in 1914 prevented an election taking place but village branches and constituency committees kept the cause alive and Charlie's position as leader became stronger than ever. He became known as the people's champion.

Distressed as he was by the high rate of casualties on the Western Front, he had a particular compassion for bereaved parents and wives whose army allowances quickly ceased on their loved one's death, but who found the bureaucrats cold and obstructive in the payment of pensions. Charlie spent generously of his time and money fighting for the rights of these dependants. Frequently a distressed wife or mother would come to see my mother and ask, 'Please write a letter to Charlie White for me'. They had great faith in his efforts to get justice for them. No wonder that when an election was announced they were all keen to do anything they could to help Charlie, and to support their hero, Lloyd George, who they thought of as 'the man who won the war'. He now wanted to build 'a land fit for heroes'.

At the end of the hostilities it was necessary to have an election as Lloyd George's coalition of some Liberals, some Conservatives and a few Labour members had kept itself in office long after the statutory period, and in any case, the Labour members withdrew immediately. Three days after the signing of the Armistice it was announced that Parliament would be dissolved on 25 November, and an election would take place on 14 December. Lloyd George's aim was to strengthen his position as leader of a coalition for post-war recovery. It was complicated by the fact that both Liberals and Conservatives were split into different wings supporting or opposing the coalition.

Locally it was a time of frantic activity. With only a fortnight for the election campaign there was no time to set up a village committee room. So our cottage became the Liberals' headquarters. There was a constant stream of callers – some to address envelopes. I did my share of this. The candidate and his agent called, and my father and his friends cycled round the adjoining villages, canvassing. At some risk to himself, Charlie even went to the estate village of Edensor, inside Chatsworth Park, to try to persuade the workers that they should not vote Tory just out of loyalty to their employers.

There was a great bitterness between Tories with their blue rosettes, and the Liberals with their yellow rosettes. Neighbours refused to speak to one another for months afterwards. My father was particularly scornful of working people who were over-awed when the Duchess of Devonshire came to the village with Lord Kerry (a Cavendish cousin) who was the Tory candidate. They put up Union Jacks, and one neighbour even decorated his wall with his prized aspidistra plants in case the gentry should pass by.

Instead of calling strike meetings my father and the rest of the cobblers held Liberal meetings and endeavoured to get support from young men who had not voted before. There were many of these as an Act of Parliament had given the vote to all men of twenty-one years and for the first time some women had the vote. This was limited to women of thirty years and over, but only if they or their husbands owned property. (Throughout the country 6 million men and 2 million women had the vote for the first time. It was impossible to predict what the result would be.) Though my mother and most of her friends were not qualified to vote, this did not prevent them from working as hard as the men for the Liberal cause.

On Election Day ill-feeling between the rival parties was intense. There was the rare sight of a motor car transporting supporters of Lord Kerry to the polling-station at the village school. The Liberals responded by borrowing a horse and trap from a local farmer, and festooning it with yellow ribbons. As it drove through the street with Charlie's followers, it was the target of much jeering and barracking, especially from the shoe-factory bosses, who were hobnobbing with the gentry, and wearing blue rosettes as big as dinner-plates. They were supremely confident that the Liberals were 'no-hopers'.

At the end of the day the ballot boxes were taken by post van to the local market town, and there locked up for safe keeping by the police. Though the election took place on 14 December the votes were not counted until 28 December, to give time for the collection of votes from members of the armed forces, many of them still overseas. In the event only one in four of these registered a vote.

Snowstorms and icy gales persisted over Christmas. The carol singers had to reduce their usual programme, but the traditional yule-log gave welcome warmth. By 28 December many roads were blocked by snow-drifts, but somehow my father got to Matlock to observe the count. It was a long day for those waiting at home, but when at last news got back to the village, the results were beyond the wildest dreams of the Liberals:

Charles F. White (Lib.)	10,752
Lord Kerry (Con.)	8,592
Liberal majority	**2,160**

Charlie, the people's champion, had unseated the aristocratic Tories, who had held the West Derbyshire seat for as long as anyone could remember. No wonder his faithful supporters took to the streets with such heartfelt emotion that tears and laughter were equally evident. Their jubilation was complete when two days later the *Sheffield Independent* had the news that Lloyd George was once more Prime Minister. Of course everyone wanted a victory demonstration, but on that New Year's Day of 1919, grimmer matters intervened.

It was a typical Peak District winter. Roads were blocked by snow-drifts and people were having to be dug out of their homes. The strike was causing grave hardship, and worst of all the flu epidemic was claiming victims daily. Several Liberal supporters died; most were ill. But spring came at last. The snow melted and the mountain streams and the River Derwent became rushing torrents. The invalids emerged into the wintry sunshine, and the time had come to honour Charlie's triumph.

Before Easter it was all arranged. Short though money was, with so many existing on strike pay (or less) and many facing big doctors' bills for wives and children in the aftermath of the flu epidemic, these warm-hearted people collected the large sum of £57 for Charlie. They knew that, as a poor man, it would be difficult for him to afford to live in London on the MP's small allowance. The money was changed into gold sovereigns and put into a purse. The people who years before had fêted Uncle Billy Gowland on his return from the Boer War had not forgotten how to create a celebration.

As it was to be a winter evening event they organized a torch-light procession. We children were allowed to stay up for this memorable part of the proceedings. Half the village semed to have gathered in the Town End. First came Eyam Band, then a horse-drawn carriage for our MP and Mrs White, followed by all the Liberals carrying home-made torches. I still remember the bituminous smell of flickering lights and the smoke as these torches were carried on long poles cut from fallen tree branches. We marched the mile length of the village and back, singing, shouting, and laughing.

Our defeated political rivals kept their doors firmly shut and maintained an angry silence. Then, when the children had been sent home to bed, the faithful crowded into the Mechanics Institute. Every seat, every window ledge, even the edge of the platform held jostling bodies. There were musical items, speeches, and finally the presentation of the purse to Charlie, with some suitable gift to Mrs White.

When the programme was over, Farewell Barnes, Tommy Barber and some of the young fellows climbed to the top of Sir William Hill and ignited the bonfire they had built the previous weekend. It was the traditional climax of a Peakland celebration.

It was an evening of excitement and rejoicing. The working people had challenged the rich and powerful, and had triumphed. I think they felt that if they could do that they could do anything. They came back to their industrial dispute with more determination than ever.

I cannot judge whether the election results were a good thing for the nation, or not. In our remote village we were little concerned with the intricacy of party politics, or the Irish Question. We were aware of the post-war slump, and the millions of unemployed. When groups of ex-soldiers, many of them crippled, appeared in the village as beggars, we sympathized, since we shared the same hardships. Two measures were introduced which slightly relieved our destitution. In 1920 unemployment insurance was extended to cover all workers earning less than £5 a week, except civil servants, domestic servants and agricultural workers. This covered 12 million people and was funded by contributions from employers and workers. It did not help long-term unemployed, as no one could receive this small payment unless they had a certain number of stamps on their cards.

Then in the mid-twenties came the first national health insurance, run on the same principle. Benefits were small, but when added to Friendly Society payments this helped to avoid utter penury when a workman was ill. However, there were many gaps. Wives and mothers were not provided for at all except at times of child bearing. Children under five were left out, and during their school years they were only inspected, seldom treated, by the school medical and dental service. Of the adult population, only wage-earners were included in the national health insurance, which meant that not only dependants were left out, but also independent workers, and it was not until 1938 that youths of fourteen to sixteen years were included.

For my family, living was still precarious. We dug our allotments, gathered our bilberries and blackberries, helped to raise funds for St Dunstan's (a charity for blinded servicemen), and for hospitals. Walking in the Peak District became more popular as a Sunday occupation, so there were more customers for mother's pots of tea, bread and home-made jam. Father found odd jobs, and we managed.

Some of the shoe operatives who were on strike became weary and hungry and drifted back to the factories which were existing on blackleg labour. But my father and his friends refused to surrender without union recognition. They held meetings and rallies, listened to stirring speeches from visiting officials from other unions, and made no progress at all. As hope of success faded, it became more urgent (and more difficult) to find a regular job, if only to get some precious stamps on an insurance card. This led to a painful choice. My father was inhibited by a fanatical devotion to his locality, his village, and to the cottage where he was born. The idea of leaving it to look for work elsewhere was unthinkable. But when a friend found him a job in Sheffield he knew that this was the only way out of our financial predicament.

So father became a labourer in a foundry, filling moulds with sand, and gasping in the heat and stench, as molten metal was poured out from the great crucible to make wagon wheels. He was on nights, regularly, 6.00 p.m. to 6.00 a.m. six shifts a week. He found cheap lodgings with friends in a terraced house in Sheffield's east end. Here he slept in the morning, often disturbed by barking dogs, shouting children and other work-a-day noises. On fine days he would walk in the local park in the afternoon, or he would read in the local library, or look at the shops.

No wonder he treasured his weekends in his beloved country. After finishing his shift at 6.00 a.m. on Saturday, he would wash and tidy himself, and catch an early train from Sheffield to Grindleford, usually walking the last 4 miles home. Then he could take off his shoes, and sit by the shiny grate with its blazing fire, and for an hour or more he would talk. I suppose I was about thirteen years old, and this was the highlight of my week. I listened spellbound as he described the great foundry, or the wonder of the new Woolworths store, or recounted the books he had read. He became engrossed in popular science, and amazed me with predictions of aeroplanes which would fly around the world, and machines which would enable us to see, as well as hear, scenes from far countries. It all sounded incredible. I liked it best of all when he told me of the fiction he had read. Rider Haggard and Conan Doyle were among his favourite authors, and while mother was busy with household chores he retold their exciting stories. He would be so carried away with *King Solomon's Mines*, or *Around the World in Eighty Days* that he would have to be reminded to go to bed to catch up with his sleep.

Though he spent little, he enjoyed looking at the city shops, especially Woolworths, with its concept of 'Nothing over sixpence'. He described its multitude of bargains as though it had been an 'Aladdin's Cave' of treasure. Sometimes he bought a couple of pieces of leather to mend a pair of shoes. He bought himself a much needed pair of spectacles, sometimes he bought us a few sweets, and at Easter he delighted and surprised us with two Easter eggs of thin chocolate, with the names 'Doris' and 'George' written in white icing sugar. George soon ate his, but mine was displayed in a mug on the organ for many weeks, and only occasionally did I have a little nibble from the plain side at the back.

My father continued to work in the foundry until 1929, living in Sheffield during the week and coming home at the weekend. He found the work unpleasant, and it was to have a long-term ill-effect on his health. But we had some financial security, although his income was decreased by lodging and travelling expenses. He would have loved to have found a job in the country, but his former employers used their influence to prevent that. They expressed some satisfaction that he had been forced to leave the village to work, but they would have been happier to get rid of the whole family from the area. They had one more try to punish him for daring to oppose them.

I have said that our cottage had been occupied by our family for at least three generations, but we did not own it. We paid rent to the Oddfellows Friendly Society, which had invested in a number of cottages in the village. These properties were managed by a board of trustees, quite separately from the local 'club'. There were seven trustees, three of whom were owners of shoe factories, and three others were their close friends. They devised a scheme to evict my father from his home. Of course the rent had been paid regularly, and the Friendly Society could not be associated with such treatment of a member. But if the house was sold, the new owner could demand vacant possession in those days. The tenant had no redress. So in 1922 it was announced that Laurel Cottage was to be put up for auction. In the present time of greater mobility, it is difficult to understand the fierce attachment a man could have for one poor cottage, or to understand his deep emotional distress when he told us, 'They are going to sell my home over my head'. He took time off to attend the auction on 13 July 1922. After all the years of low wages, and then of almost destitution during the strike no one believed that he had any savings. My mother saw him go, with a heavy heart, and his enemies had already decided which of their friends should put in a winning bid for the property. He had in fact a little nest-egg hidden away, secretly accumulated from a lifetime of thrift and penny-pinching. I never knew how much this was, probably £90–£100, but a good cottage could be bought in those days for £60–£80. It ought to have been enough. There was some surprise when he started the bidding, but the other people at the sale were money men, determined to outbid him. So the bids went up and up, until at last it was knocked down to my father for £240, three times its value. It was a wicked scheme to be rid of him. There was some amusement when he went forward to put down a deposit. It was believed that he was bound to default, and bring greater disgrace on himself, for before the days of easy mortgages and bank loans, there was no way that he would have access to that kind of money. He came home and wept, and we all wept with him.

I never knew where he eventually got the money. It was probably lent by his elderly aunt, who was of a similarly thrifty disposition. All I knew was that the cottage became ours, and we were one of the few working-class families in the village to own property. And for years later father was niggardly with money as he struggled to pay off the secret debt.

So he continued his foundry work, joining in local activities at the weekend, still interested in the Liberal Association, the Friendly Society, the Band of Hope, and village sports and festivities. In his weekday absence my mother took over the newspaper reporting, political duties, and fund raising for St Dunstan's Institute for Blind Servicemen, hospitals, the nursing association and the like. It was a busy life, and at fourteen years of age I was completely involved.

Meanwhile, by the end of the summer of 1922 the political scene in the country was in turmoil. Both the Liberal and Conservative parties were split, and Lloyd George was finding it impossible to hold his coalition together. He was subject to intense pesonal attacks, especially when his scandalous 'sale of honours' was revealed. In the autumn, the Conservatives, led by Bonar Law, pulled out of the coalition, making a General Election necessary. Parliament was dissolved on 26 October and the election took place on 15 November 1922.

The problem for the local Liberals was whether they could get their hero, Charlie White, re-elected. This time there seemed even less hope. Lloyd George, the Welsh wizard, was losing his magic, and the local Conservative candidate was Lord Hartington, eldest son of the Duke of Devonshire. No member of the Chatsworth House Cavendishes had ever been known to fail to be elected.

Though my father could not be so active in the cause because of his work in Sheffield, my mother and all our friends more than made up for his absence. The meetings and canvassing were just as enthusiastic as in 1918. Father came home to vote on election day, which saw the first change to wintry weather. It was bitterly cold for the elderly to come out to vote, and at the end of the day blizzards of snow began to fall as the ballot boxes were collected. It continued all night and next morning, falling to great depth, with huge drifts, so that only by tremendous efforts were all the boxes collected, making a count possible the following day in this rural area.

This time we did not have to wait for newspapers for news of national trends, as for the first time overnight General Election results were broadcast on the radio.

Few village people had radio sets, and even they were still only to be heard on headphones. I had learned about radio from some of the young ramblers who called on Sunday for mother's pots of tea. First a young man presented me with a crystal and cat's whisker, and I learnt to make a primitive set. Father was delighted with this wonder of modern science and encouraged me to go further. It may seem an odd hobby for a fourteen-year-old girl, but I soon became regarded as an expert. I was able to build a valve set, using a cigar box as the base. I became adept at winding the coils which moved past one another to pick up the sound waves. High tension and a low tension batteries were needed. The high tension was provided by a number of ordinary torch batteries, linked in sequence. The low tension battery or 'accumulator' was of the wet plate type, like a small car battery. It had to be taken 3 miles to the nearest garage to be charged periodically.

With this equipment my father and several other committee men determined to keep abreast of the election results. Much to mother's disapproval it was decided that I was the best person to have the headphones, so she and my brother went to bed, and I sat at the big kitchen table in the newly-installed gaslight, with a log-fire crackling, and five solemn men sitting around with their glasses of ginger wine. As I heard results from the various constituencies in my headphones I repeated them, and father and the others tried to write them down. News came slowly at first, quickening up about 2.00 a.m. so that I found it difficult to relay them in time.

As the night wore on our gloom became deeper, as the message 'Conservative gain' was repeated time after time. It was evidently a disaster for Lloyd George and his party and our little group were staggered under the blow. I was glad when I was allowed to take off my headphones and go to bed. (We were to learn a few days later of the extent of the landslide. The results were: Conservatives, 347; Asquith Liberals, 60; National (Lloyd

George) Liberals, 57; Labour, 142. Winston Churchill was one of the Liberals to lose his seat.)

The next day someone arranged a conveyance to Matlock for the West Derbyshire count. Road conditions were terrible when father set off, taking my eleven-year-old brother with him. It was dark when the party returned, two recounts had been needed but the result was:

Charles F. White (Lib.)	13,061
Lord Hartington (Con.)	12,971
Liberal majority	**90**

Charlie was in again! It was the first time that a Cavendish had been defeated on his home ground. But Lloyd George, who Macmillan called 'The greatest War Minister since Chatham', left Downing Street, never to return. Bonar Law was the new Prime Minister.

We had the usual victory celebration, somewhat curtailed because of the severe Peak District snowstorms. And life went back to normal. Charlie went back to the Commons and continued his devoted service to the community, working tirelessly for widows, the poor and disabled war veterans, but it was not to be for long.

Throughout the country the effects of the post-war slump had brought misery and unemployment to millions, and there were voices calling for an end to our traditional free trade, and the imposition of 'protection' to rescue jobs. Within a year another election was called on this issue. It was held on 6 December 1923, once more in the depth of a Derbyshire winter. Charlie White stood as a Free Trade Liberal. He struggled with his campaign to the scattered villages of that wild area, in the bitter weather. He had worked beyond his strength and he became suddenly ill on Saturday 1 December. He had pneumonia, and though he rallied a little on the Monday, he collapsed and died on 4 December. The election was then declared void.

On a local level, I have never since known such a depth of private grief for a public figure. At his funeral thousands wept in the pouring rain. Though the local Liberal party continued, the heart had gone out of the workers. When the ensuing election was held with a new candidate (W.C. Mallinson) Lord Hartington was returned with a majority of 453. It was the end of the Liberal challenge.

CHAPTER NINE

Breaking Down The Barriers

Plan more than you can do, then do it.
Bite off more than you can chew, then chew it.
Hitch your wagon to a star.
Keep your seat and there you are!

Source unknown. A favourite saying of H. Dawson

So far I have said little about going to school. Perhaps this is because in my early years my parents had a much greater influence than my teachers who, with one exception, I regarded with very little affection.

At the age of five I started to attend the village Church of England school. It was a low stone building, with a row of smelly earth closets at the back and a stony playground in front. Separate cloakrooms for boys and girls were situated at either end. Each had a row of pegs, a table with a tin bowl and a piece of carbolic soap, a bucket of cold water, a ladle, and a piece of towel which was only white on Monday morning, and was used as rarely as possible.

There were four classrooms. Boys and girls from five to seven years old were in the Infant Room. There were iron-framed dual desks, and we wrote with chalk on tatty squares of black cardboard, or squeakily made our marks on slates. Here two unqualified young women teachers struggled to impart the rudiments of reading and numbers.

The seven and eight year olds were in Standards one and two in a second classroom. Standards three and four shared a classroom towards the front of the school, separated by a folding partition of glass and wood from the room of the headmaster, who taught Standards five, six and seven, aged from eleven to fourteen.

Doris with her parents and godmother, 1908

I do not remember how I learned to read, but I could certainly do so before I started school. I remember little of my time in the Infants, except the name of the little boy who sat behind me and pulled my ringlets and chalked on my back. I was bored with having to copy individual letters and numbers and repeat the sounds the letters made. I believe I was fidgety and untidy, and a bit of a nuisance.

I was passed from one teacher to the other, and finally sent to Standard two with children a year older than myself. This was a little better. The teacher was a tall gentle widow with steel-grey hair, who allowed me to do sums and read books. I liked her lessons on home management, which were about wartime economies. She showed us how to make a hay-box to keep food simmering, and so save fuel. We learnt to screw newspapers into small tight coils to save coal, and were shown how to light a fire with the previous day's cinders. She was not too sure of her facts, and frequently asked our opinions on the best way to do things.

I was barely eight years old when I was transferred to Standard three, with children a year older. This was worse than any warnings had prepared me for. We were in a long narrow room with long desks with fixed seats with inkwells which were filled on Monday mornings, and a shelf underneath for books. A gangway separated our class from Standard four, and in front of that class was a blackboard and easel and a teacher's high chair. My only advantage was that I could eavesdrop on the work being done by the older class.

The teacher, who I will call Mrs B., was a massive woman who spent most of her day sitting up in her high chair. She only descended to write on the blackboard. Each child had to take work out to her, always in fear of the ruler she kept beside her. She was uninspiring and humourless, and I found the contrast painful when I thought of the fun and laughter of my parents and their friends. In fact, the only member of staff known to joke was the headmaster, 'Dicky' Owen, who was headmaster when my father was a schoolboy, and was then near retiring age. I later wondered whether he ever regretted spending his lifetime in the unrewarding task of working in this remote village. I am sure he would have been capable of greater things.

I was unhappy most of the time. I hated writing with pen and ink. My inkwell always overflowed, the steel nib of my pen was usually crossed and my neighbour nudged me. The result was that the pages in my exercise book were smudged, blotted, and spattered, and spoiled with crossings-out. Mrs B. made no effort to read my work, but daily rapped my knuckles and sent me back to do it again with painful fingers. I would get my sums right, but again would be punished for untidiness. I would let my attention stray to what the other class was doing, and was puzzled by the teacher's lack of skill in arithmetic. One day I incurred great anger. Standard four were

Family portrait, c. 1912. Doris is proudly displaying her toy-watch birthday present

doing long division sums, and the example Mrs B. had written on the blackboard was obviously wrong. Tiresome child that I was, I put up my hand and said so, and told her the correct answer. I was slapped mercilessly, and told to attend to my own work, but I noticed that she rubbed the offending sum out.

Then there was needlework, which was to be my downfall. Two afternoons a week the boys went to the headmaster's room for drawing lessons, and the senior girls joined us for one session of knitting and one of sewing. For knitting I was given a ball of black wool and four thin steel needles to knit a black sock or stocking. (We all wore hand-knitted black stockings in those days.) Someone cast the stitches on for me, but I made little progress. My small fingers had great difficulty in managing four needles at once. I lost stitches, and dropped whole needles-full, then spent ages picking them up. Some would always be missed, then the work would have to be undone and re-started. At the end of an afternoon my work would have grown very little, and would usually have less stitches on than when I first started.

But sewing was even worse. Our first task was to sew a pillowcase by hand. We were each given a piece of cheap stiff white calico, a fine needle and white cotton, and were supposed to do French seams and fine hems. We were given nothing to cover our inky desks, so my material became stained and grubby before I started. I had difficulty in threading my needle and found it hard to push through the stiff material. I always pricked my fingers and added bloodstains to the general messiness as the cotton became greyer or blacker in my sticky fingers.

The consequences were inevitable. More blows on the knuckles with the ruler, and the task of unpicking the stitches and starting again. At each effort the work became dirtier and the hand more painful, after applying more bloodstains as the knuckles bled. I usually arrived home in tears. My health began to deteriorate. I could not sleep or eat and was always restless. I developed a stammer and nervous movements of my hands and legs.

Fortunately the school medical officer came to make his annual inspection. Mother asked to see him. I suppose I was near to a nervous breakdown, caused partly by malnutrition and strain at home, partly by my troubles at school. The doctor was most concerned and described my condition as St Vitus Dance. He suggested tonics and a long break from school.

So began a glorious couple of months running wild. I climbed the hills and explored the woods, picked oak-galls, wild flowers and various tree leaves. I brought home beetles and lizards and caterpillars in matchboxes, and a hedgehog that I kept as a pet. I helped with the housework, tried to play the organ, and walked with mother to the surrounding villages to

A school photo with brother George, c. 1918. The school-wear was typical of that worn when money was scarce

collect news items for the local paper. Although I was not supposed to do any school work I read anything I could beg or borrow. I even asked the rector's wife to lend me books of verses, and memorized reams of them. I was later to recite these at concerts and local chapels and halls.

At last I became stronger. I'm sure that mother sacrificed her own food to buy special titbits to tempt me to eat. Before I returned to school mother visited Mr Owen at his home. She was worried by my apparent failures, but he reassured her by saying that I had wooden fingers, but a good head! Most of his problems were with pupils with wooden heads. He assured her that he would personally keep an eye on me. There were to be no more lessons with Mrs B. and no more needlework.

So I found myself in the big room with the big children. Dear Mr Owen – his kindness made school a pleasure for the first time. I had permission to fit in with any work I could do with the older children and to ask for help with anything I could not understand. He gave me a copybook, a non-spill inkpot and a supply of new pen nibs to practice handwriting in my own time. He never scolded, but taught me that only by being my own critic could I improve. My writing never became beautiful, but soon it was neat and legible.

I enjoyed doing more advanced work, and if at first I felt intimidated by being with older children, I need not have worried. Discipline was quiet, but firm. A leather strap hung on a hook on the master's desk. It was not used very frequently, but boys caught fighting or bullying or swearing in the school, playground or even on the way home, were sure of swift punishment. Two strokes on the left hand was the usual portion, but on a couple of occasions I remember really naughty boys having strapped bottoms.

Down one side of the room sat five or six huge boys, farmer's sons who walked daily from Foolow, a couple of miles away. They were surprisingly docile. At lunch time, when the rest of us went home, they sat in the school porch with lumps of cheese and thick slices of bread and butter. A pail of clean water stood by the headmaster's desk, with an enamelled mug nearby. This was the only drink available.

Some children came from remote farms over the moors near Bretton. In spite of the long walk in all weathers, they were rarely absent. But one twelve-year-old boy from that area regularly played truant. He would leave home at the correct time, then lose himself on the way and spend the day in any boyish escapade he could find. Eventually his father received an official complaint about his non-attendance. He was a man of fiery temper. We were shocked one day to see Billy coming down the village street tethered with reins, with his father behind him wielding a horse-whip. At the school door he handed him over to Mr Owen, saying 'I've brought him here, now

Eyam school, 1921. Back row: Herbert Richardson, Clifford Rider, Ivor Farer, George Cocker. Middle row: girls, Betty Marples, Sarah Purseglove, Ada Lowe, Lottie Ridgeway, Doris Dawson; boys, Alfred Waterhouse, Steven Bramwell. Front row: seated, Ella Willis, Mr R. Owen (Headmaster), Doris Dane

you wallop him too'. Billy got no more beating, but after that he arrived at school, alone.

Pupils stayed at the village school until the age of fourteen, but they could be given permission to leave at thirteen–and–a–half years if they had a job to go to. A few fortunate ones, with well-to-do parents, left at eleven years of age and became boarders at Lady Manners' Grammar School at Bakewell. This was a fee-paying school, but about that time they were offering a few scholarship places to children from poorer families. As I approached my eleventh birthday Mr Owen suggested to my parents that I should be entered for the examination. My mother was enthusiastic, hoping that I could be given a chance of a better education than she had enjoyed. I could not at the time understand the attitude of my father, who responded angrily. 'Don't put ideas into her head', he said, 'They'll never let her go'.

In spite of family friction I was entered, and was taken to Bakewell to sit with about thirty other children to do my examination papers. On 24 July a letter from Lady Manners School arrived. I had passed! The letter read:

You have been awarded a free place in this school, subject to the confirmation of the Board of Governors. There will be no fees, books will be found, but no railway fares will be paid. Please get your parents to fill in and sign the enclosed application and return it at once. The certificate of good conduct from your headmaster can be sent later.

The mention of railway fares was a nonsense. There was no railway or any other form of public transport between Eyam and Bakewell, only a market-day bus on Mondays. When mother wrote to point this out they replied:

It would be possible for your daughter to enter as a boarder. We are very full, but it would be possible to manage it. I enclose a prospectus, from which you will see that the fees at £15 per term; there are three terms a year of 12 or 13 weeks.

£15 a term! Well over a pound a week. With my father still without a job our whole family income was no more than that. It was impossible. 'I told you so', said father. But mother frantically tried to find a way out. Could she get me a bicycle and let me cycle the 8 miles each day, at least in summertime? Could she get me cheaper lodgings with acquaintances in Bakewell?

The idea of a young girl cycling alone each day was unrealistic, and was rejected out of hand by the school authorities. So was the suggestion of living in cheap lodgings. The final letter from the bursar put an end to my hopes:

In reply to your letter respecting your daughter, I must call your attention to the clause in the Scheme of the School which states that the School is open to boys and girls who are residing with their parents or guardians, or near relations within degrees of kindred to be fixed by the Governors, or are boarding in the house of any master or mistress.

Your daughter would not be allowed to board with any stranger in Bakewell and if you cannot comply with the school regulations you must consider the free place cancelled. I shall be glad to hear at once whether you can comply with the above rule, as the free place must be offered to the next on the list.

Yours truly

C J. Bowmar
(Bursar and Clerk to the Governors)

Of course, we had to refuse. All I had to show for my efforts was a certificate from the Derbyshire Education Committee, dated May 1919, to say that I had reached the required standard in the minor scholarship examination.

My father felt humiliated. He thought of his ex-employers, who paid to send their children to high schools, without any tests. They would smile at the outcome of his effrontery in trying to get his daughter similarly educated. People should not have ideas above their class!

Mother was distressed, but I was filled with rage. Doors had been shut in my face because we were poor, and even because I was a girl. I knew several boys who cycled daily to Tideswell to the Boys' Grammar School there. It was the spark for a lifelong anger against the injustice of any system which denied education on the grounds of class, poverty or sex.

I was persuaded to sit the exam again the next year when I was twelve, but I did not expect any better conditions. This time I was offered a free place in a choice of three schools, at Bakewell, Matlock or New Mills. The upshot was inevitable. No public transport was available to any of them, and

The certificate awarded to Doris by Derbyshire Education Committee in May 1919

there were no offers of help to pay expensive boarding fees. So once more I was deprived. I had day-dreamed of being a teacher, perhaps because in those days I was not aware of any other career open to ambitious girls. But with no hope of a grammar school I seemed destined to drift into any menial work I could find in the village.

Meanwhile I continued to educate myself under Mr Owen's guidance. I realize now that my education was entirely unstructured. Though I did some work with the older pupils, most of the time I was taking any books I fancied from the headmaster's cupboard. No doubt they dated from his student days and were old-fashioned, but I read indiscriminately: history, geography, botany, Shakespeare, Dickens and Scott. I found books of arithmetic problems which I enjoyed, and asked for explanation of simple algebra.

So time went on until I approached school-leaving age. The shoe manufacturers were still suffering from the unresolved strike and were desperate to obtain cheap female labour. My father received an indirect message to say that he could have his old job back if he would denounce the union, and take me to work in the machine room when I was thirteen-and-a-half years of age. He sent a furious reply to this attack on his principles. Both parents were adamant that I should never work in the shoe factory. Mother said that even domestic service was better than that. That prospect did not please my father who repeated his oft-quoted determination of 'never touching his forelock to the gentry'.

Once more it was Mr Owen who saved the situation. About that time a pupil teacher's centre had been set up in Bakewell. Here classes were held all day on Saturday for young people who wished to be uncertificated teachers. The students spent the rest of the week in their own village schools, studying half time and helping the teachers half time. They had one weekday off to recompense for the long day's work on Saturday, but much of their free time was spent in doing homework set in the Saturday classes.

Though at the age of fourteen I could have been expected to have a job and contribute to the family income, my parents, with great self-sacrifice, agreed to forego this for the next four years. So, in 1922 I was enrolled into the scheme. I was even paid a tiny subsistence allowance of 16s. 8d. a month (about 21p a week). This increased slightly each year.

On Saturdays we took a packed lunch, and a kind of mini-bus picked up students from the surrounding villages early in the morning, and brought us back at about five o'clock. Throughout the day we were taught a wide range of subjects by specialist teachers, most of them from the grammar school. I loved it. For the first time I handled real thick up-to-date text books of history, geography and botany, and complete works of Shakespeare.

Needlework was the responsibility of Miss Salt, an elderly lady, full of wisdom and understanding. When she realized my woeful ignorance of the subject she taught me the basic stitches using pretty canvas, a large needle and pretty embroidery threads. Soon I was cutting out and making garments with the rest of the class.

I worked hard, enjoyed my homework and got consistently good marks. Back at Eyam school during the week I was supposed to practice teaching. At first I was sent to the Infants department, but soon I was helping older children to do sums, or draw maps, and correcting their grammar and compositions. I found myself taking reading lessons with Standard five, though these children were very little younger than I was. Some of the slower readers were getting very little pleasure from the classical books they were supposed to read, so I devised a way of livening things up. I would read and memorize chunks of the books myself, then tell it as a story, stopping at an exciting incident and then would let the children read aloud. My efforts were popular, and we soon mastered *Oliver Twist, Robinson Crusoe*, and best loved of all, *Lorna Doone*. I began to enjoy the tricks of the teacher's trade.

It is appropriate here to quickly recount the rest of this episode of my life.

At the end of four years all pupil teachers sat the preliminary examination for the teachers' certificate. It was about the standard of GCSE today, except that there was no science, no languages, and only boys were taught mathematics. It was well below the standard achieved by grammar school pupils of the same age, but if we passed the examination, we could be employed as uncertificated teachers in rural schools. A few boys went on to teacher training, but it was difficult for girls to do this. We were expected to be grateful to have been educated thus far in our Saturday classes.

At the age of seventeen I wanted more than this. I was determined to go to college. Because I had once passed a county scripture exam, a local vicar thought that he might be able to get me a place in a Church of England training college for women at Derby. I am sure it was an excellent establishment, but it did not satisfy my ambitions. I wanted to go to London, I preferred a university co-educational college. When I announced this, those in authority at the centre tried to persuade me that such expectations were ludicrous. Pupil teachers would not gain entry to a university. I was faced with a barrier, just as I had been at eleven years of age. But now I was older, and convinced that barriers were there to be broken down, and stubbornly insisted that I would be satisfied with nothing less. At last, His Majesty's Inspector came from Derby to reason with me. He patiently explained that to go to university I would need to matriculate in at least five subjects, including mathematics, a foreign language and English. As I had not studied maths or French, I would have no chance.

Looking back, I wonder how I dared argue with this august gentleman, but I insisted that I could prepare five subjects. I was confident about my English, I would do history, because if the syllabus was different from the work at the centre, I could read it up. I explained that I was more competent in maths than anyone guessed, as, when I was supposed to have been drawing, I had listened in to the boys' lessons, and frequently worked out answers for neighbouring boys who were struggling. I would choose music theory for my fourth subject. No one had taught me this, but I had studied it as a hobby. That just left the foreign language. Would it not be possible for someone to lend me some French books so that I could teach myself enough to answer the written paper?

I think the learned gentleman was amused at my arrogance and optimism. I would not listen to reason, so I might as well be allowed to try, hopeless though it was. So he got me the necessary syllabuses, personally paid the fee and entered me for the exam at Sheffield University, and brought me some French primers. He even found a French teacher to give me an hour's lesson once a fortnight.

I had six months to prepare for both the exams, 'prelims' and matriculation. It meant burning the midnight oil, and reading by candlelight in bed when the rest of the family were asleep.

'Prelims' was in June and I sat with pupils of my year. With the exception of needlework this posed no problem. Then, during a July heatwave, I presented myself at Sheffield University to sit matriculation. In the crowded room of students I knew no-one. I attended on three successive days. It was stiffer than I had expected, and I was fearful about the French papers. I knew I had to gain enough marks in written work to compensate for offering no oral test. I was sure that I had failed, and on returning home I warned the family never to mention the matter again. I am told that when the results came through, mother opened the envelope. When she came to my bedroom to tell me of my success, I fainted in sheer disbelief.

So I qualified myself for higher education. There were other hurdles to overcome, mainly financial, but I filled up an application form for Goldsmiths' College (University of London) for the following year.

Meanwhile I took a post as uncertificated teacher for a year in a mining village in east Derbyshire. It was in 1926/27 and covered the period of the General Strike and the Miners' Strike, and was not a happy time. Still I was getting a gross salary of £90 a year. I had to pay for board and lodgings during the week, and fares to go home at the weekend, but I managed to

Doris aged 19, 1927

give a little to my parents, and to buy inexpensive material to make clothes. I could not save much towards college.

I was offered a place at Goldsmiths' after an interview in which the vice-principal told me that I was the first student to be accepted with no grammar school background.

Next came the problem of money, which my family was unable to provide. Not only were there no student grants in those days, but high fees had to be paid for tuition and residence. It was another example of the advantage held by students from privileged homes. The Derbyshire Education Committee generously offered help. They gave me a small special grant, and awarded me a small scholarship in recognition of my achievements. This only paid a fraction of the fees, but they granted a loan to pay the rest, on condition that I qualified, then came back to the county for three years and paid the money back in instalments, from my future salary. This money went straight to the college, so I had still no personal income.

Father was then working in the foundry, and I had persuaded him to let me go so that in later years I would be in a better position to help the family. He promised to pay my train fares to London each term, and to allow me £2 a month for pocket money and books. Of course it was not enough, but I was long used to being hard up.

So it was that in September 1927 I left my village for London and college. I had a Derbyshire accent, no money, frumpish clothes, and no aptitude for communal life, small talk or organized games. I must have seemed an oddity. But I was there, with access to culture, libraries, and scholarly discussion. And only a tram-ride away London waited to be explored.

I think I blazed a trail for other bright young people from impoverished families. Within a decade several of the obstacles I had encountered had been removed, and more opportunities created.

Most credit must go to my parents, whose self-sacrifice had made my success possible, and whose devotion and courage had inspired me. They and their friends had taught me how to survive through self-help, and to fight injustice, as they had done by their involvement in industrial action and political struggles and countless everyday difficulties. Above all their sense of humour and capacity for fun had prevented me from becoming too solemn. I think even my eccentric ancestors would have approved.

Among my father's papers I found a handwritten copy of his favourite poem, W.E. Henley's 'Invictis'. Once when his life seemed very gloomy, he quoted this to me:

A twenty-first birthday celebration with friends at Goldsmiths

In the fell clutch of circumstance
I have not winced or cried aloud.
Under the bludgeonings of chance
my head is bloody, but unbowed.

And the final defiant stanza:

I am the master of my fate,
I am the captain of my soul.

CHAPTER TEN

Destinations

*To travel hopefully is a better thing than to arrive, and
the true success is to labour.*

Robert Louis Stevenson, 'El Dorado'

My father was made redundant from the steel works when he was fifty-nine
years old. Too young to draw his old-age pension, and too old to find
regular work, it meant going back again to finding odd jobs, or drawing
unemployment pay. It was demoralizing, especially as 'the dole' was means
tested, and he was penalized for owning his own cottage. But we were less
needy than we had been in his earlier days. After regular employment for
about seven years family finances were healthier. I was in my first teaching
post and my brother had a job in the shoe factory so we were able to
contribute a little.

In every other way his early retirement was a blessing. He had no longer
to endure the heat and dirt and strenuous work of the foundry. He could
spend all his time in the village and countryside he loved so much, and in
closer companionship with my mother than had been possible when he was
travelling to Sheffield each week.

At this time the local water authority built a small reservoir up above the
village, and so it was possible for the first time to have piped water to the
houses. No more carrying heavy pails from the tap in the village square! It
was typical of father that he insisted that ours should be the first cottage to
be connected. He was asked to take on part-time work as a kind of
caretaker of the reservoir and the local water system. He enjoyed climbing
the hill to inspect the supply, keeping his eyes open for faults, advising
householders who were contemplating installing supplies. He did minor
plumbing, and fitted new washers etc. for neighbours.

It was a happy retirement. He maintained his interests. He played the
organ, or his tin whistle, conducted choirs, and listened to radio music on

117

headphones. He kept up his membership of the Liberal Association, and the Oddfellows, who honoured him with high office, and sent him as a delegate to annual conferences in London and in Eastbourne. He became a member of the local volunteer fire brigade; we had a telephone and an alarm bell to call him out in an emergency.

The game of bowls was one of his later enthusiasms, and he helped a group of his friends to level the garden of the fire station and lay down a crown green. It became a favourite social meeting-place and the scene of fierce competition. On one occasion his interest in sport was a little disconcerting. I knew he liked to go to support the village cricket and football teams, and he was delighted when he knew that a mixed hockey team had been formed. One Saturday afternoon I turned up to watch them play, and was startled to find that my pensioner father was goal-keeping for these vigorous young men and women. In spite of our protests he did this

Brother George with Patch, c. 1929 – one of a long line of canine companions

for most of a season, apparently doing a good job, and mercifully avoiding injury.

My brother and I were proud that he lived to give his blessing to our respective marriages. The onset of his last illness coincided with the outbreak of the Second World War. Mother nursed him till he died, in his own home, in March 1940, at the age of sixty-nine.

Mother stayed on alone in the cottage till her death at the ripe old age of eighty-four. She was sustained and supported by my brother, and Nellie his wife, who lived nearby. She remained active, in spite of an arthritic hip, and maintained her sparkle and cheerfulness; 'Mrs Thankful' to the end. She was rich in friends from all walks of life, welcoming the young, and writing copious letters. She tended her garden, worked for St Dunstan's and the Nursing Association, and was faithful to her Liberal beliefs. It was a red-letter day when she met and shook hands with her idol, Lloyd George, at a rally at Cliff College. She was a loving nana to her little grandsons, and enriched the lives of her son and daughter by her affection and inspiration.

My kind and gentle brother had no academic interest, and was never very robust. When he left school my father reluctantly allowed him to take a job in the packing department of a shoe factory for a few years. He was then recommended to work out of doors, and spent the rest of his life in the employment of the local council. He always kept poultry, selling his eggs and rearing his own chickens. He was popular in the village, where he was never seen without a dog, usually one he had rescued from neglect. After mother's death, he and his wife and young son moved into Laurel Cottage, but he was to die in his early fifties. The cottage is still there, being lovingly modernized and restored by my nephew.

And I survived to tell their story.

Henry, wearing his chain of office, and Margaret in the late 1930s

Epilogue

When Henry Dawson died in March 1940, the snow lay in drifts on Kinder Scout and weighed down the branches of the trees on the slopes behind the village.

In the lane the discoloured slush was churned up where the little group of members of the Wesleyan Reform Church trampled it round the door of the cottage. There was a knock on the door and a few words of condolence. Then as the bearers brought the coffin to the door, they began to sing, as they had so often sung by this door when Henry had led their choir. Then the choice had always been 'Peace o'er the Earth', and 'T'owd Virgin' (A Virgin most pure as the Prophets foretold). Today they sang 'Cwm Rhonnda' and 'Abide with me' and the chapel superintendent added an extempore prayer before Henry was finally carried from the cottage where he had been born, and where his mother and grandparents had lived before him.

He was carried to rest in the old style, with no cars or hearses, but borne on the shoulders of six youngish men who were neighbours, or sons of Henry's friends. They had been chosen carefully, and 'bidden' by the bereaved family. All deemed it an honour to pay their last respects in this strenuous way.

Behind came the little group of family mourners. Margaret Dawson and her son George, her daughter and son-in-law, George's wife, Nellie, and one or two cousins. But in the lane a score of men were waiting to join the cortege. They were fellow members of the High Peak Lodge of the Royal Order of Oddfellows, wearing the funeral regalia, aprons and armbands. Two by two they joined the procession, some carrying wreaths for which there was no room on the coffin. So they came to the village street, between the grey stone houses, with their windows obscured with white curtains closely drawn as a sign of mourning.

As the church bell tolled its single melancholy knell others joined the funeral walk. There were neighbours and bowls players and choir members. There were old-age pensioners and children, former cobblers and officials from the water works. The Liberal candidate and his agent were there as the long procession came through the village square, up past the school and into the church.

APPENDIX ONE

Friendly Societies

1.   These early working–class organizations were the spontaneous creation of the men who became their members. This accounts for their diversity – the Buffalows, Foresters, Oddfellows, etc., The Manchester Unity Order was active as early as 1814, and by 1875 was third largest in England. It was a huge organization, made up of many independent local lodges each with its own rules, and with stirring names, for example, the Determined Lodge at Stoney Middleton, the Royal George at Castleton, the Invincibles at Holmesfield, the Inkerman at Great Longstone and the Perseverance at Taddington (all in Derbyshire).

2.   To become a member certain qualifications were required. Below is a quotation from the Rule Book of the Determined Lodge of the Grand United Order of Oddfellows at Stoney Middleton in Derbyshire in 1880:

Character of candidates for admission.
Rule 14. That persons to be eligible for admission into this society must be sound and healthy, and industrious men between the ages of eighteen and forty years and not subject to any disease calculated to prevent them from following their employment or shorten life; they must be proposed and seconded on a meeting night by some responsible members of the lodge to whom they are well known, who shall pay two shillings and sixpence proposition fees. The candidate must present himself to the lodge surgeon before he is admitted; and if the result proves satisfactory the initiation may take place the following lodge night.

Elsewhere I have read that membership could be refused because of an 'immoral' character or if his wife was not in good health.

The successful candidate was brought by his sponsors for the initiation ceremony; it was solemn, rich with ritual and symbolism. It was also so secret that only an Oddfellow would know the details and he was forbidden to disclose them.

3.   The Friendly Societies made a great contribution to social life as well as filling an economic need. They also had a considerable educational influence. They encouraged adult education through the maintenance of 'Mechanics Institutes', with their libraries, reading rooms and classes. The societies also arranged lectures and published a quarterly magazine.

4.   In the years before the first National Health Bill the national insurance scheme established by the societies was a revolutionary concept, and it must have saved lives as it enabled men to have medical treatment when they would have been prevented from doing so by poverty. The 'Lodger Surgeons' (the doctors who accepted the scheme) were great benefactors of the movement, for they did not raise their panel fees for many years, and could have made little profit. (This system, which was developed by the Friendly Societies, became the basis of our modern social legislation.)

In 1911, when Lloyd George was the Chancellor of the Exchequer, the first National Health Act not only adapted their experience to this first national insurance scheme, but also included the Friendly Societies and unions as instruments of administration. (This was the second piece of social legislation introduced by Lloyd George. In 1908 the first Old Age Pension Bill, which was not contributary, had given men over 70 who were unable to work 5s. a week, with 7s. 6d. for a married couple.)

The Act of 1911 differed from the Friendly Society schemes by being compulsory. For the first time deductions were to be made from wages (4d. a week) and the employers were compelled to contribute 5d. a week to the welfare of their employees. There was opposition from the medical profession and the employers, and also from many workers, who saw compulsory deductions as 'robbing the poor'. Fortunately the bill became law, laying the foundations for our modern National Health Insurance.

5.   For four generations the male members of my family have been active Oddfellows. In the nineteenth century my grandfather, George Dawson, was a member of the Determined Lodge at Stoney Middleton and, till his death in 1897, was well known in the organization in the Baslow district. I have found the rule books he left a good source information.

My father, Henry Dawson, was a member of the Loyal Peak Miner's Lodge at Eyam from about 1890 till his death in 1940, and held various high offices both at a local and district level. My brother, George H.B. Dawson, was initiated as soon as he was old enough (about 1930), and he in turn introduced his son, Michael (my nephew), who still keeps up the family tradition.

6.   There is still a thriving lodge in Eyam, fulfilling an important function in the context of the modern Welfare State. It now meets in the Royal Oak.

Chapel Anniversary Hymns

Hymn sung at Stoney Middleton Wesleyan Reform Chapel Sunday School Sermons, 13 July 1890:

Sabbath schools are England's glory,
Let them spread on every hand,
They send forth the Saviour's story
To the thousands of our land;
Sabbath scholars should be heedful
Of the blessings they enjoy;
God will send them more when needful,
And will all their wants supply.

Sung at Eyam, about 1900:

Our pastor and our teachers stand
Like palm-trees in an Eastern land,
Our waymarks o'er the desert wide,
At once our shelter and our guide.
Oh! may we children whom they train
In God's own pastures, count it gain
To dwell within his sacred fold,
and ne'er forsake it when we're old.

Sung at Foolow in 1890:

My Peaceful grave shall keep
My bones till that sweet day
I wake from my long sleep,
And leave my bed of clay.
My Lord, His angels shall
Their golden trumpets sound,
At whose most welcome call
My grave shall be unbound.

Often the hymns pointed to the better times in a future life, as in this verse
from the same period:

Fight on! March on! there are loved ones gone before,
Fight on! Fight on! till the strife is o'er,
Press on! Press on! till you reach the shore
And rest in glory, glory evermore.

Or this verse of a hymn about Sunday school teachers:

But when these friends of infancy
We join in happy worlds above,
Our songs shall be more sweet, more high,
Inspired with rapturous love.

The Temperance Movement

It is difficult for us to appreciate the appalling extent of poverty and drunkenness in the late nineteenth and early twentieth centuries. The novels of Emile Zola tell of squalor and debauchery in France, and in Paris in particular, as bad as anything depicted by Dickens or Hogarth. The United States had its problems, too, and attempted to solve them by prohibition in 1920. It is well known that this led to evils as great as those it set out to cure, and it was the Liberal Democrats who repealed the amendment in 1933.

In England the arguments and propaganda went on for a generation between advocates of prohibition, licencing reform and total abstinence.

Certainly drunkenness had been a great scandal between 1870 and 1910. This was not just the view of the Temperance Movement and Nonconformists, but also the verdict of historians. Sir Robert Ensor, in the *Oxford History of England (England 1870–1914)*, says:

> . . . the Balfour Act of 1904, though a great measure in its way, was all too slow to reduce the monstrous evil of intemperance – how monstrous it is difficult for this present generation to realize.

John Morley, MP, said in 1892:

> The temperance question is the deepest moral question that has stirred the hearts of mankind since the anti-slavery movement.

Even members of the liquor trade on Peel's licencing commission in 1908 said:

It is undeniable that a gigantic evil remains to be remedied, and hardly any sacrifice would be too great which would result in a marked diminution of this national degradation.

(They still rejected controls, however.)

These following extracts from the writings of Archdeacon Farrar in 1894 are typical of much of the literature on the subject of temperance even in the early twentieth century:

The fact must never be left out of sight that alcohol is one of the most lethal agents which, like every other poison, creates and constantly intensifies a craving for itself. A man who gets fond of it and does not exercise over himself a powerful and vigilant self-control, may never get drunk, and yet may expend on unnecessary drink a positively shameful proportion of his earnings. How many thousands of working men are there who see their wives and their children sink step by step into beggary, while they pour into the till of the publican the money which would make themselves and their families happy and respectable.

The room of the drunkard is often like the lair of a wild beast. It is dirty and ugly and bare. Quarrels and recriminations make it hideous. Oaths are often heard in it. Shrieks and yells and the sound of brutal blows and kicks are familiar there. The wife sits cowering and trembling as she sits at midnight listening for the heavy foot of her husband coming drunk from the gin-shop, with anguish and fury in his heart and sees the shipwreck of all decency caused by the depravity of a drunken life. Infants are over-laid by drink-sodden parents on Saturday nights. The wretched children rush away shrieking from the threats and violence of their parents. Fires of hell are burning in these hearths.

He compares this scene with the home of the total abstainer:

Bright, pretty and clean because he can afford beautiful, though cheap and simple plants on his window-sill, beautiful prints on his wall. his shelf full of noble and favourite books.

Such a style of writing does not inspire much confidence in the reader. The pomposity and self-righteousness often found were even worse:

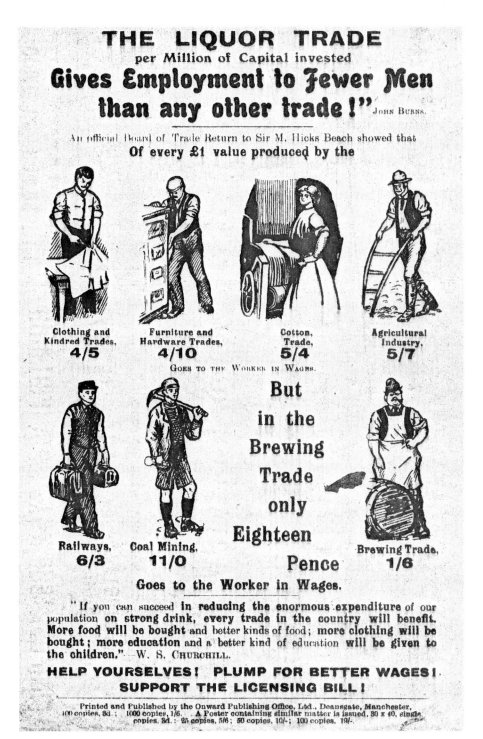

An advertisement calling for support of the Licensing Bill

I deny that the Temperance Movement has a single feature of fanaticism; for it is based on physiological principles, chemical relations and the welfare of society, the laws of self-preservation, the claims of suffering humanity, all that is noble in patriotism, generous in philanthropy and pure and good in Christianity.

William Lloyd Garrison in 'The British Workman', 1890

Perhaps an attack on the causes of poverty would have been more credible, but this would have offended the vested interests of the employing classes.

Question to the House of Commons

The following extracts are as quoted from the records of NUFLT:

26 August 1918
Col. William Thorne, MP
To ask the Minister of Labour whether he is aware of a dispute in the boot and shoe trade which has been in existence more than 16 weeks past in connection with certain firms in Eyam, near Sheffield; what action, if any, has been taken by the Department to bring about a settlement; whether either side have offered arbitration; whether arbitration has been refused, or the offers of the Ministry been turned down; and if he will take action in the matter?

Mr G. Roberts, MP, Minister of Labour
The Department recently made enquiry into this dispute. The Department offered their services in endeavouring to arrange a conference between the parties to the dispute at which it was proposed that an officer of the Ministry of Labour would preside. The Trade Union, acting on behalf of the work-people, have offered either arbitration or conciliation. The employers concerned were not disposed to accept the Department's offer of their services, and having regard to the fact that the Munitions of War Act do not apply to the dispute, and that no Government Contract work was involved, further action by the Dept. did not appear feasible.

Footnote on Will Thorne, MP:
Will Thorne was General Secretary of the GasWorkers' Union, and visited Eyam strikers in 1918 and 1919.

In 1899 Will Thorne, a young Birmingham-born Irishman who was working at the Beckton Gas Works at East Ham, began to organize a union among his fellow-workers. Almost completely illiterate himself, he was a member of the Social-Democrat Federation, and on founding the union he received a good deal of clerical assistance from Eleanor Marx, daughter of Karl Marx. Within four months his union had 20,000 members, and Thorne felt sufficiently strong to present demands for a three-shift system at the gasworks, instead of two 12 hour shifts, cutting the basic working day from 12 hours to 8 hours. The South Metropolitan Gas Co. at once conceded the demand, and some other gas companies followed suit. During 1889 and 1890 there was a spread of union enthusism throughout the industrial areas of England, Wales and Scotland. Gasworkers everywhere sought to secure the 8 hour day, and in several towns bitter strikes took place.

The fiercest struggle was at Leeds, where, on the initiative of Will Thorn, a procession of blacklegs, guarded by police and soldiers, was bombarded with brickbats and other missiles as it passed under a railway bridge. To the disgust of many of the leaders of the older unions, Thorne positively boasted of his part in the affray, and said he would willingly do it again. (Frederick Engels presented him with a copy of Karl Marx's *Das Kapital*, addressed to 'The victor of the Leeds Battle'.)

Thorne's union enrolled a good many workers in trades which had nothing to do with gas, e.g. woollen workers in the West Riding of Yorkshire.

Thorne's contemporaries and associates were Ben Tillett, Thomas Mann, James Sexton, and John Burns, all 'socialists' (Marxists), and young, militant and aggressive.

In the 1920s Thorne was active in the amalgamation of unions and in 1922 the Transport and General Workers union was formed. In 1924 the National Union of General and Muncipal Workers was formed by the amalgamation of several unions, the principle one being Thorne's GasWorkers' Union. Thorne became its first General Secretary.

In 1934 the veteran Thorne retired and was succeeded by Charles Dukes. By this time the Grand M.W. Union was the second largest in the country. In 1934 its membership was 269,357. By 1939 it had risen to 467, 318.

PICTURE CREDITS

All illustrations are from the author's collection except those on pp. 2, 3, 17, 43 which are reproduced courtesy of Derbyshire Library Service.